GNOSTICISM

GNOSTICISM

New Light on the Ancient Tradition of Inner Knowing

Stephan A. Hoeller

Quest Books
Theosophical Publishing House

Wheaton, Illinois ◆ Chennai (Madras), India

First Quest Edition 2002
Seventh Printing 2013

Quest Books
Theosophical Publishing House
PO Box 270
Wheaton, IL 60187

www.questbooks.net

Library of Congress Cataloging-in-Publication Data

Hoeller, Stephan A.
Gnosticism: new light on the ancient tradition of inner knowing/
Stephan Hoeller.—1st Quest ed.
    p.   cm.
ISBN 978-0-8356-0816-9
1. Gnosticism.   I. Title.
BT1390.H64 2002
299'.932—dc21   2001048901

Printed in the United States of America

CONTENTS

List of Illustrations

PREFACE

This book is a concise and sympathetic presentation of the teachings and spiritual ambience of the Gnostic tradition. In the twentieth century, Gnosticism matured from a subject of antiquarian interest to a topic that increasingly arrests the attention of persons in many places and in all walks of life. There is today in many minds an affinity with Gnosticism and an empathy with the attitudes of the Gnostics that have not been present since the times when the great Gnostic masters expounded their insight in the second and third centuries after Christ.

Only fifty years ago, the majority of those presently involved in Gnostic studies would have shied away from serious consideration of Gnosticism. Their main objections might have been: (1) that Gnosticism represents a tradition that is extinct and can only be approached historically; (2) that Gnosticism is so deeply immersed in cosmic pessimism that it is irrelevant in an age of progress; and (3) that Gnosticism is a tissue of speculative fancy unrelated to reason and experience. Let us glance briefly at each of these objections in turn.

In a certain sense, it may be said that no spiritual tradition becomes extinct. An insight that goes forth on the ocean of the human soul is like an expanding circle in a pool caused by a fallen stone; it proceeds outward forever, even when it is no longer perceptible to our senses. The wisdom of the Gnostics is rather like this; it continues to influence human thinking and intuition, whether it is acknowledged as the source or not. Much of the alternative spirituality of the West is in some way related to or derived from Gnosticism. (Notably, none other than Pope John Paul II in his book, *Crossing the Threshold of Hope* (90), acknowledges "the return of ancient Gnostic ideas under the guise of the so-called New Age.") The surviving and reviving ideas of Gnosticism are thus among us. To them we might apply another metaphor: that of a river. The nearer we come to the source, the purer is the water. If we wish to discover the Gnostic wisdom in its pristine expression, we must go to the fountainhead. This is what the present work tries to do.

The so-called pessimism of the Gnostic worldview has been a stumbling block for many critics. A century or even half a century ago, Western culture was full of hope; the expansion of science, coupled with the desire for human advancement, acted like a heady intoxicant spreading optimistic cheer. The upheaval of two world wars and the accompanying psychological wreckage have made us think again. More recent events have further exposed the fragility of the optimistic mindset. At the beginning of the new millennium, we are confronted with sobering circumstances: Aircraft that were once viewed as heralds of the "global village" have become destructive missiles; letters carried by the postal service are revealed as death-dealing devices. "We are all American at puberty," wrote Evelyn Waugh in his diaries, "but we die French"—referring to how naive optimism changes into somber realism as the result of experience. Such a maturing of our culture may make us appreciate Gnosticism once more.

In their attempts to discredit Gnosticism, its earliest and most influential critics represented it as replete with useless philosophizing and the products of an excessive imagination. These judgments were seriously challenged by some of the leading thinkers of the nineteenth and twentieth centuries. While biblical scholarship discerned much that was of value in Gnostic scriptures, existentialist and phenomenologist philosophers came to recognize the common ground that they shared with Gnosticism. In many ways, the most powerful effort for rehabilitating the Gnostics came from the great psychologist C. G. Jung, who perceived original images of the collective unconscious in the Gnostic scriptures and thus authenticated the visionary origin and content of Gnostic revelations. This last point is of singular relevance to the concerns of this book and therefore needs further elucidation.

The present work is being published almost exactly twenty years after my first major book, *The Gnostic Jung and the Seven Sermons to the Dead,* in which I explored Jung's exceptional interest in Gnosticism as well as pointed out numerous convergences between Jungian analytical psychology and Gnosticism. My work was received favorably, on the whole, by the Jungian community and is generally regarded as a pioneering study concerning Jung and Gnosticism. (One of my dearest possessions is a letter, written to me by Jung's son, Franz, dated January 3, 1989, in which he kindly thanked me for the way in which I had represented his father's position concerning Gnosticism. The letter was accompanied by an original, privately printed copy of Jung's *Septem Sermones ad Mortuos,* the treatise upon which my book was based.) In connection with these matters relating to Jung and Gnosticism, certain issues have become clear to me over the years, and they have a bearing on the present book.

Jung regarded the Gnostics as visionaries who expressed their insights primarily in the form of myths. He wished to rehabilitate the myths of the Gnostics even as he was in favor of rehabilitating other myths—a task that was largely undertaken by his associates Karl Kerényi, Heinrich Zimmer, and Joseph Campbell. Being a psychologist, Jung favored a psychological rather than a metaphysical interpretation of religious myths; this means that he was opposed to the prevailing religious interpretations of the Bible, which he considered concretistic and reductionistic. This orientation of Jung toward the meaning of myths was in considerable measure responsible for his positive interest in the Gnostics; the Gnostic myths lend themselves with great ease to such symbolic rather than literal treatment.

It is here that a certain difficulty emerges. Jung insists that his symbolic interpretation of myths makes no claim to metaphysical truth. Gnosticism, on the other hand, occupies a strange region between religion and what today is known as psychology—a region where soul and spirit meet and where dream and vision are transmuted into liberating experience. The Gnostic myths, with their powerful symbols and metaphors, invariably partake of both psychological and metaphysical meaning. Often they might appear as sorts of endless loops wherein the psychological meaning points to a metaphysical meaning that leads us back in turn to the individual psyche. Cosmology and psychology, deities and archetypes, metamorphose—at times pointing to each other, at other times merging together only to separate again. The reader of this book may be confronted time and again with the puzzling circumstance that the Gnostic mythic stories and their protagonists seem to belong to the field of depth psychology and to that of religion at one and the same time. Unlike Jung, the Gnostics make claims to metaphysical truth in the interpretation of their myths, although they also indicate avenues of interpretation that today would be seen as depth psychological. The most likely solution to this enigma is the view that the Gnostic myths may be interpreted in both an intrapsychic and an external sense, and that both interpretations may be correct and can coexist with each other. Both the metaphysical and the psychological models are perhaps, as Jung would certainly agree, merely attempts to formulate, express, and shape the inexpressible. It would be wise if the reader kept these considerations in mind while reading this work.

This book is not primarily a work of academic scholarship. I have tried to limit references and documentation to an irreducible minimum while expanding the list of recommended reading and annotating it for the reader's convenience. The format and style of this book are rather more simple than those of my other books, even simpler than I like. The reason for this is that the book aspires to serve as an introduction to the subject. Gnosticism is not only for the learned or the pious. Like other esoteric systems of teaching, it might be likened to an ocean, wherein a small child may wade in the shallows while a deep-sea diver may penetrate into the depths. Still, it is impossible to write a book that could bear the title *Gnosticism for Dummies*. The subject is not one that lends itself to an all too elementary treatment; rather, it requires a certain subtlety of thinking and a proclivity for an intuitive perception.

A word may be said about illustrations. Given the brevity of its history of open activity and its long underground existence, Gnosticism has very little sacred art it can call its own. It is quite likely that there were Gnostic icons and that these were destroyed during the persecutions. The cupidity of the persecutors did not, however, permit them to destroy large numbers of talismanic gems of Gnostic provenance. These contain designs showing symbolic forms, often depicting beings mentioned in Gnostic myths. The majority of these gemstones are in private collections and are not available for purposes of reproduction. Fortunately, an anonymous friend has allowed me to reproduce likenesses of some of the designs found on the gems in his collection, and some of these are reproduced in this book. There is not much else that can be illustrated that is genuinely Gnostic, save some historic places, and portraits of persons involved in the later Gnostic movements.

The title of this book describes it as containing insights into a tradition. This is intended not as a mere figure of speech, for Gnosticism is truly a tradition and not a mere collection of ideas, myths, and symbols that may be interpreted according to any whim or opinion. What we have here is a full-blown tradition with its definite worldview, its scriptures, its mystery rites, its priesthoods, and its spiritual lineage. If Gnosticism were purely a form of spontaneously motivated spirituality, unmediated by tradition, there would be no need for a book such as this. Such, however, is not the case, and therefore this book is now offered to the consideration of the reader.

Acknowledgments

Grateful acknowledgment is made to John Algeo for suggesting the writing of this book; to Sharron Dorr and Anna E. Urosevich of Quest Books for their help; to an anonymous friend in the state of Ohio for permission to reproduce part of his collection of Gnostic gems; to Obadiah Harris, president of the Philosophical Research Society, for permission to reproduce the image of the late Manly P. Hall's Gnostic ring; to Jay Kinney for permission to reproduce material by the author of this book originally published in *Gnosis* magazine; to the *Quest* magazine for permission to reproduce material by the author originally published in it; to Paul Kienewicz for the gift of several of his photographs of Montségur castle; to the late P.-E. de La Tour for the gift of pictures of Cathar monuments and designs as well as designs relating to vestments of the original Gnostic Church of France; and especially to Bryan Campbell for his invaluable assistance with the manuscript and illustrations of this work.

CHAPTER ONE

Light from beyond the Veil

O ne of the oldest and grandest inducements to philosophical thought and mystical insights is the mystery of the night sky. Long before astronomy disclosed the vastness of space, or the brilliant birth of new stars along with the ominous presence of devouring black holes, men and women looked at the dark, star-encrusted vault of the heavens and drew inspiration from that vision. One of the images arising from the contemplation of the night sky is the contrast of the innumerable points of light with the heavy blackness upon which they seem suspended. A dark bowl or lid seems to cover our world, enclosing us in dense, oppressive opacity. Yet this inverted sphere is riddled with specks of light that are easily imagined as perforations in the black veil, hinting at a boundless world of light from where the light of the stars proceeds.

"There is a crack in everything; that's how the light gets in"—so sang Leonard Cohen in "Anthem." His simple metaphor might easily have been uttered two thousand and some years ago by the unusual and ever-fascinating people who came to be known as the Gnostics. Derided and persecuted as heretics, the Gnostics were reduced to a tenuous existence after the first three or four Christian centuries, yet their teachings and practices have continued to surface throughout the history of Western culture. No sooner are Gnostics and Gnosticism declared defunct than they reappear, changed in form but undiluted in substance. While consistently represented by its enemies as a historical oddity of purely antiquarian interest, Gnosticism has attracted friends and even followers of the stature of Voltaire, William Blake, W. B. Yeats, Hermann Hesse, and C. G. Jung, to mention but a few. Among philosophical tendencies, existentialism owes much to Gnosticism, and today an increasing number of folk in many walks of life profess to being Gnostic. At the beginning of the third millennium of the Christian era, it seems that the Gnostics have returned and that this time they intend to stay.

The terms *Gnostic* and *Gnosticism* are derived from the Greek word *gnosis,* which is usually (albeit somewhat misleadingly) translated as "knowledge." For a long time, most people were more familiar with the antonym of *gnostic*—namely, *agnostic*—meaning "someone who claims to know nothing about ultimate realities and concerns." By contrast, a Gnostic is often defined as a person who seeks salvation by knowledge. The knowledge the Gnostic seeks, however, is not rational knowledge; even less is it an accumulation of information. The Greek language distinguishes between theoretical knowledge and knowledge gained through direct experience. The latter is gnosis, and a person possessing or aspiring to this knowledge is a Gnostic. Elaine Pagels, in her noted work *The Gnostic Gospels,* indicates that in the sense that the Gnostics themselves use the term, one should perhaps translate it as "insight," for gnosis involves an intuitive process that embraces both self-knowledge and knowledge of ultimate, divine realities. The enduring vitality and appeal of the Gnostic message is primarily grounded in its affinity with the deeper strata of the human mind. A number of serious scholars, including E. R. Dodds, Gilles Quispel, and Gershom Scholem, have suggested that Gnosticism originates in the experiences of the psyche, where archetypal psychology and religious mysticism meet. No wonder the great explorers of the depth psychological dimensions of myth, C. G. Jung, Karl Kerényi, Mircea Eliade, and Joseph Campbell, have all evinced much sympathy for Gnosticism.

Since the inner core of Gnosticism originates in a rather specific kind of experience, it follows that those who lack this experience readily misunderstand Gnostic insights. A mistaken notion occasionally held even by scholars is that because of its diversity of imagery and mythology, Gnosticism cannot be regarded as a coherent tradition, or "ism." This misapprehension has a long history. In the second century, Bishop Irenaeus of Lyons, a fierce opponent of the Gnostics, attacked them for their spiritual and literary creativity, accusing them of producing a new gospel every day. Implicit in his statements was the view that where such a wealth of diverse imagery, myth, and teaching exists there can be no coherent doctrine equivalent to the dogma and canon of the mainstream Christian church. What critics from Irenaeus to contemporary scholars lose sight of is that Gnostic teaching is the direct result of the experience of gnosis.

Such an experience, on the other hand, seldom if ever lends itself to uniform, dogmatic formulations after the fashion of orthodox theology. Still, in spite of the refreshing absence of such formulations, there is a common or core teaching in Gnosticism that reflects a common or core gnostic experience.

Many people in recent decades, and indeed since the latter half of the nineteenth century, have turned to Eastern religions in search of teachings and practices with less dogma and more inspiration. They have probably had no inkling that just such an alternative exists closer to home and that it is called Gnosticism. Neither have they seemed aware of the parallels between Gnostic and Eastern insights into reality, the soul, and the need for enlightenment. Some of these people have been responsible for implanting ideas from the East into the minds of the Gnostics. Others have suggested, with equal plausibility, that some Eastern schools of thought, particularly Mahayana Buddhism, may have been influenced by Gnostic ideas. Once again, the most important common element joining East and West in this regard is apparently the experience of gnosis. The similarity was noted as early as about 225 A.D. by another orthodox Christian foe of the Gnostics, Hippolytus, who in his refutations of heresies wrote concerning the Brahmins of India: "They say that God is light, not like the light one sees, nor like the sun nor fire, but to them God is discourse, not that which finds expression in articulate sounds, but that of knowledge [gnosis] through which the secret mysteries of nature are perceived by the wise."

Gnosis in the East or in the West is still gnosis, and in a very real sense that is what truly matters. Contrary to the views of some, the term *Gnosticism* is not an empty box into which one can place whatever one wants. Rather, the Gnostic tradition is based on the experience of gnosis and is characterized by certain attitudes toward life and reality and by certain myths and teachings concerning the origins and nature of the cosmos and the human being that are the result of this same experience. These characteristics set Gnosticism apart as a distinct and unbroken tradition that we can define and trace throughout the ages and across many cultures.

THE EXPERIENCE OF GNOSIS

The term *gnostikos,* meaning "Gnostic" or "knower," does not seem to have been used often in the first centuries A.D. Most simply called themselves Christians, although there also existed a non-Christian school of Gnosis known as Hermeticism. It is widely agreed, however, that the people in question were aspirants toward and partakers of an experience that brought them a liberating acquaintance with Divinity and with the intricacies and predicaments of the human condition. By what specific means the knowers came by their knowledge we are in no position to recount. Jung stated repeatedly that the scriptures of the Gnostics bear testimony to mystical-psychological experiences of a very impressive order and that what was called gnosis was undoubtedly a psychological knowledge whose contents derived from the insights of the archetypal psyche. Gershom Scholem, the great scholar of Jewish mysticism, spoke of this experience as a mystical esotericism based on acquisition of a higher knowledge of things heavenly and divine. Scholem was also greatly impressed by the preoccupation of second- and third-century Gnostics with ascending through the spheres of the planets to a realm beyond the earth and the cosmos, thus returning in consciousness to their true spiritual home in the fullness of the divine Light—a return that signified redemption in the Gnostic tradition. These "heavenly flights" are perhaps the central metaphor for the liberating and sanctifying knowledge to which these people aspired.

The monotheistic religions, Judaism, Christianity, and Islam, in their mainstream manifestations have placed much emphasis on faith. "I believe" (credo) is the central affirmation of much of the conventional religious mind. In contradistinction, the Gnostic mind aspires to, and eventually attains, not faith but a certain interior knowing that liberates one from unconsciousness and eventually transports one beyond the bounds of manifest existence itself. This state very likely has certain advantages over mere faith, or belief. William James, the great American philosopher-psychologist, remarked that to most people faith means having faith in someone else's faith. In the minds of many religious folk, faith has thus devolved into a belief received second-hand from other believers, none of whom are likely to have had any experience of the object of their faith.

Faith is a very different mode from knowledge, so it is fairly easy to understand why conventional religion is so different from Gnosticism. A certain kind of faith *(pistis)* is recognized as valid in Gnosticism, but it is faith in one's experience, an abiding faithfulness that one feels toward one's experience of inner, liberating knowledge. The Gnostic divine feminine figure, Sophia, is called Pistis (Faith) because in all her adversities she remains faithful to her vision of the light.

Harold Bloom, one of the prominent present-day admirers of Gnosticism, describes the experience of gnosis in contemporary terms in his book *Omens of Millennium.* He says gnosis is a varied phenomenon. It may happen when one is in solitude, or it may come through the presence of another person. One may be reading or writing or observing an image or a natural phenomenon, or one may be gazing only inward. Music, incense, and ritual may play a significant part; indeed, the sacramental and ceremonial predilections of the Gnostics are well known. In all instances, there occurs a significant altering of consciousness that transports the knower beyond the limitations of personal consciousness and, indeed, beyond the limitations of the very world we live in. Bloom aptly characterizes the principal disclosures of the experience of gnosis as (1) acquaintance with a God who is unknown to and remote from the world, a God in exile from a false creation and (2) recognition that one's deeper nature was no part of creation (or the Fall) but was and still is part of the fullness that is God. This God is more human and also more divine than any worshipped in the world.

The early Christians used the term *gnosis* to mean knowledge by personal acquaintance. St. Paul the Apostle used the term frequently in reference to the knowledge of God that human beings may have. One of the clearest statements he made concerning the visionary and perhaps even visual character of gnosis is in his second letter to the Corinthians (4.6): "God . . . has shone in our hearts to give the light of the knowledge [gnosis] of the glory of God in the face of Christ." Another Gnosticizing (that is, akin to Gnostic) apostle was St. John, who frequently wrote of knowing *(gignoskein)* God or Christ. Anyone who reads the beautiful Gospel of John is struck by its similarity to the poetic and visionary style of the writings of the Gnostics. The emphasis of much New Testament literature on gnosis is the source of the prominence that both mainstream Christian mystics and Gnostics have given to the word *gnosis.*

An insightful contemporary scholar, Dan Merkur, in his work *Gnosis: An Esoteric Tradition of Mystical Visions and Unions,* suggests that the experiential sources of gnosis are found in two interrelated kinds of experiences. One of these is a distinct type of visionary experience that discloses ultimate realities, albeit manifest in personal mental experiences and thus varying to some extent from individual to individual. The other concerns experiences of mystical union. The Gnostics themselves did not regard these visions as extrasensory perceptions of external data existing on higher "planes," as similar perceptions were understood by nineteenth-century occultists. Nor did they regard them as allegorical representations of abstract ideas, as might have been common among the more mystically inclined Greek philosophers. Rather, the Gnostics seem to have walked a razor-edged path between clairvoyant quasi-objectivity and philosophical, allegorizing subjectivity. Thus, in spite of a common core of meaning and direction, the accounts of the Gnostics' experiences are varied and diverse.

Students of the mystical experience frequently distinguish between what they refer to as visionary and unitive mystical states, the former being descriptive, the latter denoting divine union. It would seem that the ancient Gnostics partook of both. Gnostic visions frequently included heavenly ascensions, but other kinds of visions, such as ecstatic deaths, were in evidence also. One died to the created world and ascended through the aeonial regions, engaging in discourses with the denizens of these realms. The Gnostics apparently knew these visions to be at least partly intrapsychic and gave them a special status. They described them as experiences in which the "divine spark" *(pneuma)* resident in the individual joined with the reality of the higher worlds. Like other mystics, the Gnostic seers understood the unitive experience as a conjunction *(unio mystica)* with either a divine being (Sophia, Christ) or the spiritual essence of the ultimate Godhead. The synthesis of such visionary and unitive experiences can be characterized as gnosis.

GNOSIS AND GNOSTICISM

A number of attempts have been made to distinguish between gnosis and Gnosticism. Some of these—among them the definitions a group of scholars devised at the Colloquium at Messina in 1966—were promising but proved flawed. To define Gnosticism as the sum of the beliefs of certain "second-century sects" who were "dualists, and rejectors of the world" appears neither helpful nor accurate. Neither does the definition of *gnosis* as "knowledge of the divine mysteries reserved for an elite" seem particularly informative. Some insightful scholars in the field have noted that such definitions, as well as some other statements about the Gnostics that pop up in many books, are perpetuations of the skewed perspective of Christian heresiology. From this viewpoint, one is really interested in Gnosticism not on its own terms but only as it aroused the ire of a group of fanatical persons eighteen hundred years ago. Many of the old heresiologists' statements against Gnostics and Gnosticism appear discreditable and even somewhat silly today. The notion that Gnosticism was in the main a patchwork of teachings from various sources extant at the time has been discredited. More and more contemporary scholars agree with Jung, who recognized that the Gnostic scriptures were indeed based on their authors' direct experiences with original images of mysterious beings and regions. Neither does the forthright critique of the Old Testament God, which the Gnostics voiced so frequently, appear particularly sacrilegious to contemporary people, who are often nourished on the ideas of Nietzsche or the death-of-God theologians, such as Althizer and Hamilton. In the light of the evidence now available, few would agree with the church fathers who portrayed Gnosticism as a purposefully anti-Christian heresy, a diabolic perversion of Christianity worthy of every kind of condemnation.

The heresiological bias has colored the view of most writers and preachers concerning Gnosticism for an exceedingly long time. While it is true that the anticlerical tendencies of the Enlightenment and the several occult revivals of the eighteenth, nineteenth, and twentieth centuries spawned a good deal of sympathy for the Gnostics, the old bias emanating from the early Christian critics remained. It was not until after the discovery and translation of the Nag Hammadi Gnostic scriptures (of which more is said later) that the climate regarding Gnosticism underwent an ever accelerating benign change. Now, at the outset of the twenty-first century, it is finally possible to give an exposition of Gnosticism without meeting the overwhelming opposition of the bias that has ruled our culture for far too long.

What then is Gnosticism, and what is its relationship to the experience of gnosis? Human consciousness does not function in a conceptual vacuum. Visionary and unitive experiences of the mind necessarily translate into a conceptual framework that fits their content and import. From visions and ecstasies are born religious doctrines, philosophical constructs, and theological and theosophical conceptions. It has been so ever since the times of the primeval shamans, and so it was with the Gnostics of the early Christian centuries. The difference between mainstream religiosity of whatever kind, on the one hand, and Gnosticism, on the other, lies in what happens to their respective systems after the initial codification of revelatory experiences. While conventional religions apparently are satisfied with the accounts of their founding experiences recorded in sacred scripture, Gnostics have always sought further expansions and amplifications of the initial experiences of gnosis. Gnostics were never primarily believers in someone else's gnosis but were inclined to add to the insights of their founders and teachers through their own experiences. And, crucially, such a continuing process of gnosis required a conceptual framework in which the new experiences would find their meaningful place. This conceptual framework or worldview, within which gnostic experiences have always found their place, became known as Gnosticism.

An early normative Gnostic statement defines the content and implications of gnosis:

> What makes us free is the gnosis
> of who we were
> of what we have become
> of where we were
> of wherein we have been cast
> of whereto we are hastening
> of what we are being freed
> of what birth really is
> of what rebirth really is.
>   *(Excerpta de Theodoto)*

The person who intuitively receives accurate answers to these questions has received liberating gnosis. The combination of these questions with their answers could be said to constitute Gnostic doctrine and to be the essential core not only of gnosis but of Gnosticism.

Contemporary inquirers into these matters might assume that there can be gnosis without Gnosticism, that a person can experience visions and unions without adopting the Gnostic worldview. The ancient Gnostics, as well as their contemporary followers, might respond that while this is possible, it does not lead to productive results. What is the good of having unusual experiences without an appropriate context in which to understand them? The tradition of Gnosticism developed on the basis of such experiences in the first place and is uniquely suited to facilitate further Gnostic experiences. Clearly, gnosis and Gnosticism are intimately and usefully linked and, in fact, cannot safely be separated.

Today we know that the Gnostics always emphasized understanding and the insights derived from understanding. This understanding was not common and mundane but embodied a higher knowledge, a more profound insight into things divine and human, than is ordinarily available to faith or to philosophy. Like mystics in other traditions, the Gnostics held that this saving knowledge does not arise merely from rational processes of thought based on the memorization of phrases (even though sacred) or the study of books; nevertheless, like other mystics, they composed documents amplifying their visionary insights and attempting to communicate them to others. These texts proclaim the existence of a transcendent and totally benign God, a substratum of reality that is unchanging and immeasurable, transcending any particularity or limiting imposition one might attribute to it. It goes without saying that this God image is quite incompatible with the image of an arbitrary, tyrannical personal God in whom, to say the least, good and evil seem to be liberally mixed.

From this ultimate essentiality the sparks or spirits that are the essence of human souls come forth, and to it they seek to return. Each spirit entity is a pure spark or atom of divine consciousness and is of the same essence as God. Yet though these sparks are ontologically united with the Divine, they are existentially separated from it. This separation needs to be undone, for as a biblical phrase expresses it, "our hearts are ever restless until they find their rest" in God. A certain painful, often indistinct, longing for something greater, more meaningful, and more enduring than can be experienced in earthly embodiment is the beginning of the undoing of this great separation. Liberating gnosis, resulting in transcendent consciousness, is the effective end of the separation.

Using once again the metaphor of the midnight sky, we may view the dark vault above us as a perforated veil, through the small holes of which the light of the ultimate reality penetrates our vision. Through the holes—the cracks in the universe—a transcendental luminosity enters our consciousness. This light is the light of gnosis that awakens us to possibilities long desired but not yet realized. Light calls to light, or God calls to his children, even as they cry out to him. The lid that seals in our universe is lifted and we behold the vast ocean of boundless light, of which we are the temporarily exiled sparks. Such was and continues to be the vision of the Gnostics. The essential components of this vision are few in number and simple in nature; its detailed implications are more numerous and complex. Let us turn now to the consideration of these details.

CHAPTER TWO

THE GNOSTIC WORLDVIEW

At the core of Gnosticism is a specific spiritual experience, grounded in vision and union, that does not lend itself to the language of theology and philosophy, but instead has a close affinity to and expresses itself through myth. In this context, the term *myth* does not mean stories that are not true, but rather, stories that embody truths of a different order than the dogmas of theology or the theories of philosophy. Myths were held in high regard in the ancient world. Though they lost esteem in the nineteenth and early twentieth centuries, they are increasingly being rehabilitated in our day. A minor mythic renaissance took place in the last decades of the twentieth century, facilitated largely by C. G. Jung, Mircea Eliade, and Joseph Campbell. Their work fostered the widespread understanding that the meanings present in mythologies, ancient and otherwise, could help undo the alienation and rootlessness prevalent in the individual and collective psyches of our culture. Thus today we are in a much better position than a century ago to appreciate the mythic message of the Gnostics. This chapter presents some of the principal motifs of the Gnostic myths. Since of necessity this presentation must be in prose and not in the poetic and imaginative language of the original sources, some of the appeal and beauty of the myths are lost.

GOD AND COSMOS

Most religious and philosophical systems recognize, in one form or another, that the world is imperfect. Where they differ is in what they suggest should be done about it. In many traditions, humanity is made out to be the villain. Mainstream Judeo-Christian thought, for instance, holds that the transgression of the first human pair precipitated a fall, not only of the human race but of all creation. The flaws and evils of earthly life are considered the consequences of this fall. Some extreme environmentalists espouse a position that seems like a latter-day secular translation of the doctrine of the Fall. Human beings are seen as the despoilers, the original sinners who perennially destroy the natural paradise. Gnostics have a perhaps unique and startling view of these matters: they hold that the world is flawed because it was created in a flawed manner.

Gnosticism begins with the recognition that earthly life is filled with suffering and impermanence. "Life is hard and then you die" is an adage that Gnostics agree with, although they might modify and thus offset the first part. All forms of life consume other forms to nourish themselves, thereby visiting pain, fear, and death upon one another. This truth pertains even to herbivorous animals, who live by destroying the life of plants. In addition, so-called natural catastrophes—earthquakes, floods, fires, droughts, volcanic eruptions, plagues—bring suffering and death in their wake. The more complex an organism is, the keener is its sense of suffering and distress.

To face these alarming facts squarely is not easy. Most human beings have a strong psychological need to perceive life as in some sense benign and potentially happy. Gnostics (and Buddhists) have often been labeled pessimists and world haters because of their willingness to look the dark face of the world in the eye. Yet, both of these traditions affirm that there is a way out of suffering and ignorance, and that this way out involves an essential, salvific change in consciousness.

As long as a person will not raise his or her consciousness beyond the physical world to higher, spiritual realities, the soul's enslavement in darkness—whether darkness in the outer, physical world or in the world of the mind—continues. It is as though the body and the mind were bars of a cage in which the soul (or spirit) is trapped. When the captive entity exits the cage and flies aloft, it rises to spiritual realms where ultimate meaning and happiness abide. Soaring through these regions, it finally reaches its primordial home, the Divine.

Describing Gnostics as pessimists is valid only if one maintains that the physical and personal psychological realms are the only realities. Regrettably, this view underlies much contemporary secular thought in our culture. In contrast to this view, the Gnostics assign a high value to the self-liberating potential of transcendental consciousness.

The reader may be familiar with Plato's renowned analogy of the cave. Prisoners held in the cave, being unable to see outside, mistake shadows on the wall of the cave to be reality. The light that is the source of the shadows, however, is the true reality. The Gnostics hold that humans have the potential to turn away from the shadows on the wall permanently and commune with reality directly. This is the basis for an important point: The created world, including a major portion of the human mind, is seen as evil by the Gnostic primarily because it distracts consciousness away from knowledge of the Divine. Physicality inevitably attracts one to the external (psychology calls this "extroversion"), while the turbulence of the personal mind focuses attention on itself. Through this double distraction, the inner self is forgotten. Yet it is this inner self ("spirit," Greek *pneuma*) that is the point of transcendence within the human field of experience, for it alone has a direct link with ultimate Divinity. Through the experience of transcendence, what Gnostics regard as the true "original sin," namely, alienation and separation of the human from the Divine, can be undone.

To state that Gnosticism is anticosmic, that Gnostics are world haters, is a gross oversimplification. What the Gnostic struggles against is not so much the cosmos as the alienation of consciousness from the ultimate reality underlying the cosmos, which in monotheistic language is called "God." Since to the soul without gnosis the cosmos appears to be the only reality, it is an obstacle to the Gnostic's true objective, which is the raising of consciousness above all physical and mental substitute realities to the true reality, beyond matter and mind.

The ancient Gnostics lived in a largely monotheistic milieu. The Jews and Christians, and even the pagan Hermeticists, believed in a singular God. Monotheists envision God as the creator and usually also as the sustainer, lawgiver, and law enforcer of the universe. Since the Gnostics—rather reasonably, it seems—could not believe that an erring pair of human ancestors could have brought about the innumerable evils and unpleasantries of the world, they were left with only one culprit: the Creator, God himself. The world did not fall, the Gnostics said; rather, it was imperfect from the start.

The proposition that the world was created by an imperfect deity in its own flawed image makes more sense when one understands the Gnostic concept of God, which is more subtle than most. The God of the Gnostics is the ultimate reality, beyond and in a sense quite alien to the created universe. Like Kabbalists and most esotericists the world over, Gnostics substitute the idea of the emanation of the Divine in place of the idea of creation. The transcendent God does not create; the divine essence emanates, comes forth, from the unmanifest state into the manifest, making possible further, more specific creation. The original God remains always the first cause, while other entities become the subordinate, or secondary, causes of creation.

To use a homely analogy: A financier or landowner may decide to develop a large piece of land. Most likely this person will not be directly involved in clearing and preparing the land or in planning and constructing the buildings. Architects, engineers, construction workers, and others will do this work. Is it unreasonable to think that the world might have been created in a similar manner? The Gnostics have always held this view. To elaborate on the analogy: If the landowner becomes less and less involved in the development and the chief architect is inept and his workers slovenly, then in spite of the good intentions of the owner, the final results will be anything but perfect.

The architect was known in ancient Gnosticism as the Demiurge— from the Greek *demiurgos*, "half-maker," since he made only the form but not the inner life of the world. The workmen and future managers were called *archons*, using the Greek word for "petty rulers." It goes without saying that the majority of the deeds and words of the Old Testament God accord with the character of the Demiurge. Gnosticism's disdain for Yahveh must be ascribed precisely to this circumstance.

THE HUMAN BEING

Gnosticism holds that human beings are essentially not the product of the material world. The important term in this statement is *essentially*, for Gnosticism focuses on the essence rather than the physical and mental containers that envelop this essence. Though the theory of biological evolution did not exist at the time of the ancient Gnostics, one might guess that unlike their mainstream Christian brethren, they would not have objected to it. For they believed that the human body originates on earth but the human spirit has come from afar, from the realm of the Fullness, where the true Godhead dwells. A human being consists of physical and psychic components, which are perishable, as well as a spiritual component, which is a fragment of the divine essence, sometimes called the divine spark. Because the Gnostic tradition recognizes this dual nature—of the world as well as the human being—it has earned the epithet *dualistic*.

People are generally ignorant of the divine spark residing within them. This ignorance serves the interests of the archons, who act as cosmic slave masters, keeping the light sparks in bondage. Anything that causes us to remain attached to earthly things, including the mental concepts we hold, keeps us in enslavement to these lesser cosmic rulers. The majority of men and women are like Adam, who was asleep in Paradise. Modern esoteric teachers (notably G. Gurdjieff) have capitalized on this Gnostic theme, representing humanity as a throng of sleepwalkers. Awakening from this sleep is the combined result of our desire for liberation and the supernal help extended to us.

Gnosticism professes a very distinct and elaborate soteriology—that is, a teaching regarding salvation and saviors. The sleeping human spirit is stirred by the call of the ultimate Divine by way of divine men, or messengers of Light. Such beings have come forth from the True God throughout history. They descend from the highest spiritual realms to call souls back; they come to restore the human spirit to its original consciousness and lead it back to the Divine. Only a few of these salvific figures are mentioned in Gnostic scripture; some of the more important are Seth (the third son of Adam), Jesus, and the prophet Mani. At times a salvific role is attributed to some of the Old Testament prophets, and in the later (Manichaean) Gnostic tradition some founders of other great religions, such as Buddha and Zarathustra, are recognized as true messengers of Light. The majority of Gnostics have always looked to Jesus as the principal savior figure. Even Mani, who carried on his work in Iran and in Asia, regarded himself as a prophet of Jesus Christ and revered Jesus as the savior.

What does salvation mean to Gnostics? In many ways, the Gnostic concept of salvation is close to the concept of liberation found in the Hindu and Buddhist traditions; Gnostics look to salvation not from sin (original or other), but from the ignorance of which sin is the consequence. Those who know the Divine through gnosis shed all sin, while those without gnosis cannot help but persist in transgressions. Ignorance—which means ignorance of spiritual realities—is dispelled by gnosis. The decisive revelation of gnosis was brought by the messengers of Light, especially by Jesus, who is recognized as the messenger of this age.

The Gnostic concept of salvation is subtle. Students of spirituality whose grasp of Gnostic ideas is superficial often misunderstand salvation by gnosis as a totally unmediated individual experience, a sort of spiritual do-it-yourself project. This projection onto the Gnostic tradition is largely a product of our secular, religiously alienated age and society. Were salvation possible without any outside aid, the vast majority of the human race would have been liberated long ago. Neither is salvific gnosis the result of mere reading, intellectual speculation, and discourse. To be liberated from the predicament of spiritual ignorance we require help, alongside our own efforts.

INDIVIDUAL SALVATION

Gnosticism has always acknowledged that the potential for gnosis, and thus salvation, is inherent in every man and woman, and that salvation is not vicarious and collective but individual. Thus the entire message of mainstream Christian atonement theology is meaningless to the Gnostic. The world was not created perfect, its present state is not the result of a fall, and the human race did not incur an original sin that is passed on to all men and women. Consequently there is no need for God's son to be sacrificed in order to pacify his wrathful Father and thereby save humanity. Notably, the original Greek word for sin, *hamartia,* means "missing the mark." When used in this sense, the word *sinner* describes most people. We all miss the mark, and we do so because we are ignorant of things true and divine. The great messengers of Light come to stimulate our ability to shake off this ignorance. We need the enlightening teachings and liberating mysteries (sacraments) they bring to help us manifest our indwelling potential for liberation.

Those whom the messengers of Light awaken from their spiritual slumber—and who then put forth the required amount of spiritual effort and diligence—become true Gnostics (knowers, or pneumatics, truly spiritual persons), wheras others remain unconscious and earthbound. Some call this view elitist, and the contemporary egalitarian mindset tends to rebel against elitism. But there is a difference between an arbitrary, self-interested elitism that sets oneself and one's fellows apart as a chosen group, on the one hand, and the inevitable existence of elite persons, on the other. The late spiritual teacher J. Krishnamurti wrote in his little classic, *At the Feet of the Master* (6): "In all the world, there are only two kinds of people—those who know and those who do not know." No Gnostic, ancient or modern, could have expressed it better.

The enemies of the Gnostics (beginning with the heresiologist church fathers) never tired of claiming that the Gnostics were proud elitists who held the rest of humanity in contempt. Yet there are no records of Gnostic crimes against humanity—of the followers of Gnosticism tyrannizing over or persecuting those who were not of their spiritual conviction or who disagreed with them. The inquisitions, crusades, and jihads were not devised by Gnostics but were frequently devised against them.

The allegedly world-denying attitude of Gnosticism is frequently misinterpreted as conducive to suicide or other acts that injure life. Some cases of religious mass suicide in the last quarter of the twentieth century (Jonestown, the Temple Solaire, Heaven's Gate) were viewed by the public and the media as the result of Gnostic doctrines and practices. Nothing could be further from the truth. Yes, the Gnostic feels that earthly life is in many ways a state of enslavement to the dark powers, yet no Gnostic is known to have believed that death brings about automatic liberation from these onerous conditions. Liberating knowledge must come while a person is still in the embodied state, and those who attain such spiritual liberation enjoy their freedom whether they are in or out of embodiment. On the other hand, those who are not liberated in consciousness are by definition still entrapped in the shackles of manifestation, whether they are in or out of the body. Several Gnostic documents indicate that human beings repeatedly return to this earthly realm (that is, they reincarnate) until their transformed consciousness makes rebirth no longer necessary.

When Confucius was asked about death, he replied: "Why do you ask me about death when you do not know how to live?" To a similar question posed in the Gnostic Gospel according to Thomas, Jesus answered:

> Know ye then the Beginning so that you inquire about the End? For where the Beginning is there shall be the End. Blessed is the man who stands at the Beginning, for he shall know the End, and he shall not taste death. (saying 18)

The implications are clear: the Gnostic needs to know the eternal realm from where souls originate. This knowledge makes all issues of life and death self-evident and takes away all fear of what the world calls death. When we are in contact with the ineffable, divine reality that is our source, we also know what state we shall return to. Without this knowledge we are indeed dead, even though we may show signs of physical life. From this standpoint, suicide—religiously or otherwise motivated—appears as a singularly counterproductive act.

In addition to being accused of spiritual elitism, Gnostics have also time and again been charged with advocating moral nihilism, known technically as *antinomianism*, or "opposition to the law." Here also the subtlety of the Gnostic position is easily missed. Most religions teach that people attain salvation by obeying the rules (for instance, the laws of Manu, of Hammurabi, or of Moses) revealed by a divine or quasi-divine source. This position clearly lacks psychological refinement. People do not act in a vacuum; a person's conduct rises out of his state of consciousness. Murder is the result of a murderous state of mind, lying is the manifestation of a lack of integrity and authenticity in the mind and soul. Buddha, the great Gnostic of Asia, stated that right thinking must be present for right action to occur. Gnosticism is a system of thought based on interior, psychospiritual experience. This being the case, it is not surprising that Gnosticism emphasizes states of mind and regards actions as secondary in nature and importance. Gnostics have always held that consciousness, rather than external action, is the true indicator of moral worth.

If ethics and morals are taken to refer to a system of rules, the Gnostic is not likely to regard them very highly. Rules without the consciousness that reveals the reason behind the rules are little better than useless. Thus many Gnostics say that rules and laws in themselves are not salvific, for salvation comes only by gnosis. On the other hand, if morality is defined as an inner integrity rising from the illumination stemming from the indwelling supernal spark, it is likely to be enthusiastically embraced by followers of the Gnostic tradition.

This sketch of core ideas of Gnosticism may give rise to some questions about interpretation and application. As we saw earlier, in a sense there is no gnosis without Gnosticism, for the experience of gnosis inevitably calls for a worldview appropriate to its insight. The Gnostic worldview is experiential, for it is based on a specific kind of experience. Because of this it will not do to omit or dilute parts of the Gnostic worldview, for then the worldview would no longer conform to the experience.

Gnosticism originates in a specific and particular kind of experience. So also, Gnosticism as a worldview is distinct from other forms of mysticism. There are similarities, to be sure, between the recognitions of St. John of the Cross or St. Theresa of Avila and the mysticism of a Gnostic seer, such as Valentinus, but St. John and St. Theresa share a Roman Catholic worldview (albeit one with which ecclesiastical bureaucrats are often somewhat uncomfortable), while Valentinus is distinctly Gnostic in outlook. Despite the common elements that unite various traditions, the distinctive, indeed at times, unique characteristics that divide them are significant and valuable.

We live in an eclectic age. Just as we purchase our food in supermarkets, where choices often border on the bewildering, so we can choose our spiritual nourishment in a kind of marketplace where variety is prominent. When encountering Gnosticism at the psychospiritual supermarket, we might be tempted to accept some parts of its worldview and to discard others. We may gladly envision our true selfhood as a divine spark sprung from a transcendental fullness but have reservations about the more dark and disturbing Gnostic insights, such as the figure of the Demiurge and his malicious archons, the radically flawed nature of the universe, and the presence of evil in its fabric. The Gnostic worldview, however, is an internally consistent whole; when we remove parts of the whole, its integrity suffers.

Another important question is whether the elements of the Gnostic worldview are to be understood literally or symbolically. Literalism and dogmatism, which manifest all too often in the mainstream churches that have declared Gnosticism heretical, are distinctly un-Gnostic views. Gnosticism has a worldview, but it has no theology and no doctrines to believe in. The Gnostic scriptures are primarily mythical in content, and all myths can be interpreted in diverse ways. Modern depth psychology, especially as taught by Jung, has explored the Gnostic myths primarily because of their relevance to archetypes, individuation, the shadow, and similar concepts. The Gnostic myths, like other myths, can hold a number of meanings that do not cancel each other out but exist simultaneously. Psychological truths, in addition to other kinds of truth, can be found in these myths, and none of these truths needs to be denied.

The Gnostic worldview holds a perennial appeal because it has always been in accord with the "knowledge of the heart" that is gnosis. Some feel that Gnosticism is especially timely at the beginning of the third millennium. The end of the second millennium saw the radical deterioration of many ideologies that could not stand up to the questions of the times; these questions, however, are addressed by the sages of Gnosticism. The clarity, frankness, authenticity, and frequently the contemporary relevance of Gnostic answers to questions of the human predicament cannot fail to impress and, in time, to convince.

A CREATIVE VIEW OF CREATION:
GENESIS REVISITED

Some years ago, Elaine H. Pagels, the scholar who has contributed more than any other to the popular interest in Gnosticism, found herself in the capital city of Sudan holding a discussion with the foreign minister of that country. This distinguished person, a member of the Dinka tribe, told her how the creation myth of his people has exerted a lasting influence on many aspects of their social and cultural life. Shortly thereafter, Pagels was looking through a copy of *Time* magazine in which several letters to the editor took issue with an earlier article on the changing social mores of America. To her surprise, many of these letters referred to the story of Adam and Eve to argue for the desirable code of behavior. The letters consistently justified the morals and ethics of present times by referring to the creation story recorded in Genesis. Not only the Dinka but also Americans were still influenced by their creation myth. Pagels realized that Americans and Dinka tribesmen are not so very different; the creation myths of both are still vital and relevant today.

Most Westerners assume that Western culture has only one creation myth: the one in the first three chapters of Genesis. Few seem to be aware that there is an alternative—the creation myth of the Gnostics. This myth may strike us as novel and startling, yet it offers views of the creation and of our lives that are well worth considering.

William Blake, the Gnostic poet of the early nineteenth century, wrote: "Both read the Bible day and night, but you read black where I read white." Similar words might have been uttered by early Gnostics about their opponents in the ranks of Judaism and Christianity. The non-Gnostic, or orthodox, view in early Christendom regarded most of the Bible, particularly Genesis, as history with a moral. Adam and Eve were historical personages whose tragic transgression resulted in the Fall, and from their Fall later human beings were to learn portentous moral lessons. One consequence of this reading of Genesis was the ambivalent and worse than ambivalent status of women, who were regarded as Eve's co-conspirators in disobedience in Paradise. Tertullian, one of the church fathers who despised the Gnostics, wrote thus to a group of Christian women:

> You are the devil's gateway . . . You are she who persuaded him whom the devil did not dare attack. . . . Do you know that you are each an Eve? The sentence of God on your sex lives on in this age; the guilt, necessarily, lives on too. (*De Cultu Feminarum* 1.12)

The Gnostic Christians, whose legacy of sacred literature we find in the splendid Nag Hammadi library, read Genesis not as history with a moral but as a myth with a meaning. They regarded Adam and Eve not as historical figures but as representatives of two intrapsychic principles present within every human being. Adam was the dramatic embodiment of *psyche,* or "soul": the mind-emotion complex where thinking and feeling originate. Eve stood for *pneuma,* or "spirit," representing the higher, transcendental consciousness.

There are two biblical accounts regarding the creation of the first woman. One tells us that Eve was created out of Adam's rib (Gen. 2.21); the other, that God created the first human pair, male and female, in his own image (Gen. 1.26–27). The second account suggests that the Creator God himself has a dyadic nature, combining male and female characteristics. The Gnostics generally endorsed this version and developed various interpretations of it. This version accords equality to the woman, while the Adam's-rib version makes her subordinate to the man.

For the ancient Gnostics, the conventional image of Eve was not credible. That image presented her as the one who was led astray by the evil serpent and who, with her feminine seductive charm, persuaded Adam to disobey God. In their view, Eve was not a gullible dunce turned persuasive temptress; rather, she was a wise woman, a true daughter of Sophia, the celestial Wisdom. In this capacity, she was the one who awakened the sleeping Adam. Thus in the Apocryphon of John, Eve says:

> I entered into the midst of the dungeon which is the prison of the body. And I spoke thus: "He who hears, let him arise from the deep sleep." And then he [Adam] wept and shed tears. . . . He spoke, asking: "Who is it that calls my name, and whence has this hope come unto me, while I am in the chains of this prison?" And I spoke thus: "I am the foreknowledge of pure light; I am the thought of the undefiled spirit. . . . Arise and remember . . . and follow your root which is I . . . and beware of the deep sleep."

In another scripture, On the Origin of the World, Eve is presented as the daughter, and especially the messenger, of the divine Sophia. It is in the capacity of messenger that she comes as an instructor to Adam and raises him up from his sleep of unconsciousness. In most Gnostic scriptures, Eve appears as Adam's superior. The conclusion drawn from these texts is obviously different from that of church fathers such as

Tertullian: man is indebted to woman for bringing him to life and to consciousness. One cannot help but wonder how the Western attitude toward women might have developed had the Gnostic view of Eve been the widely accepted view.

OF SNAKES AND MEN

Eve's mistake, the orthodox view tells us, was that she listened to the evil serpent, who persuaded her that the fruit of the tree would make both herself and Adam wise and immortal. A treatise from the Nag Hammadi Gnostic collection, The Testimony of Truth, reverses this interpretation. Far from an embodiment of evil, the serpent is considered the wisest creature in Paradise. The text extols the wisdom of the serpent and casts serious aspersions on the Creator, asking: "What sort is he then, this God?" It answers that God's prohibition concerning the fruit of the tree is motivated by envy, because he does not wish humans to awaken to higher knowledge.

Neither are the threats and anger of the Old Testament Creator God left without reproach. The Testimony of Truth tells us that he has shown himself to be "an envious slanderer," a jealous God who inflicts cruel and unjust punishment on those who displease him. The text comments: "But these are the things he said (and did) to those who believe in him and serve him." The clear implication is that with a God like this, one needs no enemies, and perhaps no devil either.

Another scripture from the same collection, The Hypostasis of the Archons, informs us that not only Eve but also the serpent was inspired and guided by the divine Sophia. Sophia allowed her wisdom to enter the serpent, who thereby became a teacher and then taught Adam and Eve about their true source. They came to understand that they were not lowly beings created by the Demiurge (in this case, the Creator in the Genesis story), but rather, that their spiritual selves had originated beyond this world, in the fullness of the ultimate Godhead.

While the mainstream version of Genesis says that after eating the forbidden fruit Adam and Eve fell from paradisiacal grace, the Gnostic version says that "their eyes were opened"—a metaphor for gnosis. The first humans could then see for the first time that the deities who had created them were loathsome in appearance, having the faces of animals, and they recoiled in horror at the sight of them. Although cursed by the Demiurge and his archons, the first human pair had acquired the capacity for gnosis. They could pass this on to those of their descendants who were inclined to receive it. Eve thus passed on her gift of gnosis to her daughter Norea, and Adam gave the same to his third son, Seth.

MYTHIC BEGINNINGS OF GNOSTICISM: NOREA AND SETH

Norea, Eve's daughter, was a wise woman. She eventually married Noah, a well-intentioned but unperceptive man. By that time, humans had proliferated and, inspired by Adam and Eve, were distrustful of and disobedient toward the archonic masters of the earth. Far from becoming wicked and thus causing God to regret his creation, as the "official" version of Genesis declares, they had become wise and were striving for freedom from the archons. Noah was told by the Creator to build an ark and place it on top of Mount Seir—a name that is not found in Genesis, though it is in one of the psalms referring to the Flood.

Norea tried to persuade her simpleminded husband to refuse to cooperate with the archons. At one point she even burned down the wooden boat constructed by Noah. The Creator and his dark host then surrounded Norea and intended to rape her as a punishment. She put up a powerful defense by arguing with them and ultimately cried out for help to the True God, who sent the golden angel Eleleth (Sagacity). The angel not only saved her but also instructed her in Gnostic wisdom and assured her that her descendants would be genuine knowers of the Truth.

Several major scriptures from the Nag Hammadi collection—The Hypostasis of the Archons, Apocryphon of John, and The Thought of Norea—make reference to the story of Norea and the ark. They agree that Noah's progeny were hidden not in the ark, as in the "official" version, but in a luminous cloud, where they were protected by the angels of the True God.

Fig. 1. Gnostic gem, circa third century after Christ, depicting Abraxas. The figure holds the traditional whip and shield, symbols of attack and defense. Surrounding Abraxas are stars with a varying number of rays as well as an eight-fold symbol of the *ogdoad*, the symbol of transcending the seven planets.

Seth, the third son of Adam (after Cain and Abel), has long been regarded as a mysterious figure. The ancient historian Josephus writes that Seth was a very great man and that he and his family were the custodians of many secret arts, including astrology. The descendants of Seth inscribed records of their occult discoveries on two pillars, according to Josephus, so that they might be preserved for posterity. In the treatise The Apocalypse of Adam, the Gnostic writers tell us not only of Seth (and his father, Adam) but of the future of the Gnostic tradition in ages to come. In this text, Adam tells Seth that it was Eve who taught Adam "the word of the Gnosis of the eternal God." He then discloses how the Creator turned against Adam and Eve, and how he was ever eager to make humans serve him "in fear and slavery." Adam then predicts that "Seth and his seed" would continue to experience gnosis, but they would also be subject to further persecution by the Creator.

Adam's prediction catalogues the two major calamities that follow: the Flood and the fiery destruction of Sodom and Gomorrah. Both come about not because of the sinfulness of humans, but because of the envy and anger of the Creator-Demiurge, who could not tolerate people acquiring Gnostic wisdom. Just as in the Flood, at the catastrophe of Gomorrah the True God sent a number of aeonial beings to save the Gnostics from the fire by taking them above the realm of the archons. Seth, who is considered the father of the Gnostic tradition, is mentioned prominently in several other scriptures, including The Three Steles of Seth and The Gospel of the Egyptians.

The extant Gnostic scriptures clearly indicate that Gnostics have always been present in the world, though they have perpetually been oppressed and frequently in danger of extermination by the dark powers, whom they have opposed from the beginning. The Gnostics, referred to as "the great race of Seth," would endure until a future era when the Illuminator (Phoster), at times identified as Jesus, would initiate a time of knowledge and liberation. The continuing struggle of the spiritual offspring of Seth is not with this church or that inquisition, but with the same metaphysical adversaries of whom The Hypostasis of the Archons says:

> The great apostle said to us concerning the powers of darkness; "Our fight is not against flesh and blood, but it is against the powers of the world and what pertains to the spirit of wickedness."

The "great apostle" is of course St. Paul, and the abbreviated quotation is from his letter to the Ephesians (Eph. 6.12).

THE NATURE OF GNOSTIC EXEGESIS

What motivated the Gnostic interpreters of Genesis to proclaim such unusual versions of the creation story? Did they wish only to bitterly criticize the God of Israel, as the church fathers would have us believe? The several possible reasons are not necessarily mutually exclusive and in some cases are complementary.

First, the Gnostics, along with some other early Christians, looked upon the Old Testament God as an embarrassment. Members of the more intellectual echelons of early Christendom were people of a certain spiritual sophistication. Those conversant with the teachings of Plato, Philo, Plotinus, and similar teachers would have had a difficult time relating to a God expressing vengefulness, wrath, jealousy, tribal xenophobia, and dictatorial pretensions. How much more compatible with the genteel philosophy of Gnosticism was the kindly and noble character of Jesus and his teachings. The Gnostics might have simply drawn the logical consequences from this dichotomy and consigned the Old Testament God to the status of a demiurge, a lesser cosmic entity.

Second, as noted earlier, the Gnostics were inclined to interpret the old scriptures symbolically. Modern theologians, like Paul Tillich, would have felt quite comfortable with the Gnostics, whose interpretation of Genesis they have often approximated. Tillich says that the story of the Fall was a symbol for the human existential situation, not a recounting of a historical event. The Fall, he writes, represented "a fall from the state of dreaming innocence," a kind of awakening from potentiality to actuality—an interpretation not unlike the Gnostic one we considered earlier in this chapter. Similarly, Tillich endorses a concept closely resembling the Gnostic idea of "two Gods" when he speaks of "the God above God."

Third, the Gnostic interpretations of Genesis may have been connected with Gnostic visionary experiences. Through their explorations and experiences of divine mysteries, the Gnostics might have come to understand that the deity spoken of in Genesis was not the true and only God, contrary to what the Bible claimed, and that there must be a God above him.

A transcendent God, minimally involved in the creation and management of the world, would have been plausible in the eyes of many people living in the Greco-Egyptian-Roman milieu of the first centuries of the Christian era. The highly personal and painfully flawed God of the Old Testament had lost credibility even with many Jews, as the example of the philosopher Philo of Alexandria proves. This learned man, though a devout Jew, employed his talents in whitewashing the concept of the God of Israel by investing it with Platonic ideas. These included divine hypostases (emanated aspects of the Deity) such as the Logos and Sophia, both of which were held in high regard by the Gnostics. Taking an even more radical and forthcoming stand, the interpreters whose words are contained in the Nag Hammadi scriptures reasoned that a God who behaved as Genesis and other books of the Old Testament described must be a pretender and a usurper, not worthy of worship or obedience.

The Gnostics understood the creation story in Genesis as mythic, and myths are necessarily subject to interpretation. Greek philosophers frequently looked upon their myths as allegories, while the common people saw them as a sort of quasi-history, and the *mystae* (initiates) of the Eleusinian and other mysteries brought the myths to life by way of visionary experiences. There is no reason to believe that the Gnostics approached myths in a manner substantially different from these.

Present-day liberal biblical scholars tend to view the biblical tales as mythic stories that people invented to try to explain the world around and above them. If this view is accurate, then the contradictions in the creation myth of Genesis are no more than reflections of the contradictions implicit in life generally. But the Gnostics, along with many other mystical philosophers of the ancient world, viewed mythic reality differently. They were more interested in understanding and realizing the world within than in explaining the world around and above them. The world within pointed to the world beyond, to transcendence, which was all-important. The myths of the Gnostics are designed to stimulate experiences in which the individual soul transcends the world's limitations. To transcend, in their view, means to go beyond the limitations not only of materiality but also of mind. It is in the realm of psyche that contemporary psychologists have discovered the analogues of what the Gnostics called the archons and the Demiurge. As C. G. Jung differentiated between the Self and the ego—the two "gods" in the psyche—so the Gnostics spoke of two gods, one transcendental, the other a bumbling secondary deity. Depth psychology seems to shed more light on the Gnostic understanding of the Judeo-Christian creation myth than liberal biblical scholarship does. Even so, there are probably meanings in these mythologems, or mythological themes, that elude the grasp of both psychologist and Bible scholar.

It is relatively easy to perceive the Gnostics as blasphemous religious deviants as long as one does not think too deeply and logically about the nature and implications of such scriptures as the Book of Genesis. It is also not difficult to convince oneself that the reprehensible character of the Creator described in these scriptures is in no way compatible with that of the Father of Jesus. The two-Gods doctrine of Gnosticism certainly speaks more clearly to the ethical and logical sense of the human mind than does mainstream Judeo-Christian monotheism with its desperate desire to gloss over the glaring contradictions alluded to here.

As the child is father to the man, so the creation myths of various cultures leave their imprint on the histories of peoples and nations. The Gnostics apparently made a valiant attempt to free the youthful Western culture of their time from the shadow of the Judeo-Christian creation myth. If the alternative myth they suggested seems radical to us, it is only because we have been accustomed to the Genesis version for so many centuries. Many of the implications of the Gnostic version are in fact potentially useful for the culture of the twenty-first century. Perhaps the time has come to transvalue the Western creation myth, and if so, Gnosticism may serve as our helper and ally.

SOPHIA: GNOSTIC ARCHETYPE OF FEMININE WISDOM

The phenomenon of exile has become tragically familiar in our era of history. In the course of the second half of the twentieth century, millions upon millions of people were herded from or forced to flee from their ancestral homelands to spend their lives in places and among persons who are alien to their race, their traditions, their very souls. Deportations, ethnic cleansings, refugee camps, and enclaves of exiles desperately trying to preserve vestiges of their ancient cultures are familiar and ever-reappearing realities at the outset of the twenty-first century. The legacy and horror of exile are ever with us.

The Gnostics recognized the condition of exile as more than an event of history. They saw it as having a profound cosmic and even transcosmic dimension. The human spirit, they held, is quite literally a stranger in a strange land. "Sometimes I feel like a motherless child," laments the American spiritual. The Gnostics would have agreed—and might have been tempted to replace "sometimes" with "always."

In the Gnostic view, recognition of our alienness in this world is not an occasion for sorrow or a reason for psychological chaos, as might be the response in today's secular society. The forlornness of exile is not an enemy, said the Gnostics. Alienation and forlornness are our friends, for they point to a necessary truth that demands our awareness. Most people are like the "Philistine" Kierkegaard speaks of, who "tranquilizes himself with the trivial," but the Gnostic cannot pursue such a course. The exile may indeed find himself in a dark land, but his very awareness of the darkness can also reveal a light on the path to freedom. So also, awareness of our alienness and recognition of our place of exile for what it is are the first great steps on the path of return. We begin to rise as soon as we realize that we have fallen.

SOPHIA: GREATEST OF EXILES

The predicament of exile and alienation is not confined to humanity, nor does it originate at the human level. Long before there were men and women, long before there was a cosmos as we know it, a great drama of exile and return was played out in the story of the divine feminine being named Sophia. Having resided in the lofty height of the eternal Fullness *(Pleroma)* in the embrace of her aeonial spouse, she leaves her original habitat and descends into realms of chaos and desperate alienation. From the Gnostic scriptures, we learn that Sophia is the youngest of the great beings who populate the Fullness. As such, she is far removed from the primal light of the Father, who is the central and essential source of all. Sophia had seen a light in the distance that she thought might be the Father, but it was only that Light reflected in the depth of the Abyss. Seeking the Light, she journeys farther and farther into the deceptive depths, until she is at last stopped by a power known as the Limit *(Horos)*.

At this point a strange division occurs within Sophia's nature. Her higher self, her essential core, becomes enlightened and mystically ascends back to the Fullness, while her lower self remains in alienation. In virtually all Gnostic myths, an intimate relationship exists between the nature and condition of the human soul or spirit, on the one hand, and the transcosmic archetype, on the other. Thus we understand that our own consciousness has emerged from a primordial wholeness and proceeded into alienation and chaos. Yet even in our confused state,

Fig. 2. Icon of the Holy Sophia, the Wisdom of God. Sophia is shown as a winged, crowned woman, in red robes and with red hair. She is flanked by the Virgin Mary and St. John the Baptist, who stand on platforms at a level lower than her own. Seven streams of power proceed from her throne, and above her are Christ and six angels. (Russian, nineteenth century; possession of the author.)

we still sense a connection, no matter how tenuous, with a higher, transcendental self. Thus, like Sophia, we are split in two: our human personality abides in confusion and alienation, while our eternal self partakes of wholeness and wisdom.

The lower Sophia, Achamoth (an anagram of *Chokmah*, the Hebrew name for Wisdom), struggles in her alienated condition. She grieves and rages; she sorrows and longs for her original estate. In her distress she manifests, or emanates, powers that eventually condense into the building blocks of the material universe—envisioned in antiquity as earth, water, fire, and air. She also produces a hybrid form of consciousness, a lion-headed, monstrous being who becomes the Demiurge (also known as IALDABAOTH, Saclas, and Samael), the "Artificer" of the created world. Sophia's misbegotten offspring proceeds to design his own kingdom, which is composed of seven spheres (planets), presided over by seven rulers *(archontes)* of time, who are the rulers

Fig. 3. Contemporary Gnostic icon of Sophia. The figure is crowned and winged and has before her a world tree with the serpent of wisdom, holding an apple. (Oil painting by John F. Goelz; by permission of the artist.)

of destiny and the jailers of spirits. Sophia in her lower selfhood remains ensconced in the eighth sphere, above the seven.

The internal or, as some have called it, the ontological side of these mythologems was always present in Gnostic thought. The church father Hippolytus in his discussion of this myth states that in the Gnostic system "the Sophia is called 'pneuma' [spirit] the demiurge 'soul.'" This and similar statements suggest that this mythology is applicable to the human psyche. The lower, psychic nature, with its ego-consciousness, is certainly a mental artificer par excellence, imposing its own order on life and reality. We organize our own cosmos (or create our own reality, as some would have it) and at the same time impose our own flaws on it. The division of Sophia's being into lower and higher selves is reflected here: the human being's lower self (the psychological ego) appears as the Demiurge, while the higher self or spiritual soul appears as Sophia.

Critics of the Gnostics have frequently alleged that Sophia's demiurgic offspring is evil. An informed reading of the Gnostic scriptures reveals, however, that the chief characteristic of this entity is ignorance, not evil. The texts say repeatedly that he is unaware of anything above him. Thus he is ignorant of even his own mother's existence. This is somewhat of an advantage, however, because it allows Sophia to insert her own design into creation, which he believes he has made by himself. The created world thus becomes a mixture of the flawed work of the Demiurge and the celestial wisdom and beauty of Sophia. The heresiological church father Irenaeus, describing the Gnostic view, writes that the Artificer believed that he manufactured these things by himself, unaware that [Sophia] Achamoth worked through him. In addition to ignorance, the Artificer is also filled with conceit and presumption. He believes that he is alone or, in his own words, that "he is the only God and that there is no other God above him." Sophia angrily contradicts him, saying that there are indeed other, superior powers above him and that he is but a minor figure within a greater scheme. The Demiurge, however, keeps this information to himself and continues to let the creatures he reigns over believe that he is the true and only God. Once again, the ontological or intrapsychic analogy holds true: The ego, or lesser self, is generally ignorant of the deeper powers within the collective unconscious (to use Jung's model); and the more the ego becomes alienated from the archetypal matrix from which it originates, the more it is likely to assume that it is the lone determining agency of its own existence. The egotism of the ego is thus the interior corollary of the arrogance of the Artificer.

RETURN OF THE EXILE

The fall and exile of Sophia do not remain unnoticed. The divine inhabitants of the Fullness, as well as the Fullness itself, are distraught at her exile. Together they appeal to the ultimate Godhead, and he gives them a warrant for her redemption. A number of the high Aeons of the Fullness, including the Holy Spirit, the Christos, and Jesus (destined to become the outer manifestation of the Christos), join forces in a mission of rescue. The powers of the Fullness also pool their strengths and fill the rescuers with invincible light and perspicacity.

The Christos appears to Sophia in the shape of a form stretched out on the transcosmic tau cross. The vision of this cross blazing and radiating through the aeonial regions vitalizes Sophia and infuses into her a tremendous longing for her celestial home and her divine bridegroom. Metaphysical and intrapsychic elements conjoin powerfully in this portion of the myth. The disturbance of the Fullness and the unhappiness of the divine beings over Sophia's plight reveal the Gnostic awareness of a mystery—not only does the exiled soul long for the Fullness, but the divine beings also long for the return of the soul.

Heaven is not complete until the exile has returned from the far country; until then, the Fullness is not truly full, the Wholeness is not truly whole.

It is no doubt psychologically significant that Sophia's first awakening from unconsciousness occurs through the archetypal symbol of the cross. In the process of individuation, the psyche is often prepared for the coming interior liberation by experiences of numinous symbols, mandala designs, and the like. Perhaps the conjunction of the horizontal and vertical bars of the cross even reminds the psyche/Sophia of the needed conjunction of the opposites.

Slowly and laboriously, Sophia ascends toward the light of the Fullness, traversing the twelve regions that she had transgressed—in the literal sense of "passed through"—on her way down into chaos. To undo these transgressions, she utters twelve "repentances," or poetic statements, which allow her to rise through the twelve gates, as they are sometimes called. She cries out to the twelve powers in elaborate ritual supplications addressed to the ultimate Divinity, here always called Light. The poetic and mystical-magical qualities of these formulas are clear even in brief samples, such as the following:

> Rescue me, O Light, from the lion-faced Power and from the emanations of divine Arrogance; for it is Thou, O Light, in whose light I have believed, and I have trusted to thy light from the first. . . . It is Thou who shalt save me. . . . Now then, O Light, leave me not in the Chaos. . . . Do not abandon me, O Light, for . . . they have desired my power, saying to one another all at once: "The Light has forsaken her, seize her, and let us take away all the light in her."
>
> Let those who would take my power be turned to the Chaos and put to shame, let them be swiftly turned to Darkness . . . let everyone who seeks after the Light rejoice and be glad! . . . Thou, then, O Light, Thou art my Saviour. . . . Hasten and save me from this Chaos.
> (Pistis Sophia, chapter 32)

In ever-ascending circles, Sophia approaches the world of the Light, guided and aided by angelic and archangelic powers, and strengthened by the force infused into her by her heavenly bridegroom, Jesus. Joy now replaces the deep anguish and dejection of her earlier repentances as she addresses the Light:

> I have been rescued in the Chaos and loosed from the bonds of Darkness; I have come to Thee, O Light, for Thou hast become Light on every side of me . . . and the emanations of the Arrogant one which opposed me Thou hast hindered with Thy Light. . . . Now hast Thou covered me with the Light of Thy Stream and hast purified in me all evil matters. . . . I have become encouraged by Thy light . . . and have shone in Thy great power, for it is Thou who savest always!
>
> The Light has become Saviour for me and has changed for me my darkness into light: He has rent the Chaos that surrounded me and girded me with light! . . . All powers that are in me, sing to the Name of His Holy Mystery . . . which has filled thee with refined light. (Pistis Sophia, chapter 32)

Even at this juncture, Sophia's enemies have not abandoned their pursuit of her. They continue to attack and trouble her right up to the threshold of the highest aeonic home of the Light. Then the dark powers suddenly fall away, and she enters the kingdom of the boundless Light. Praising the liberating glory of the Light, she bursts forth once more into a paean of praise:

> O Light, I shall disclose how Thou hast saved me, and how Thy wonders have taken place in the human race! . . . Thou hast smashed the high gates of Darkness together with the mighty bolts of Chaos . . . and I have come up through the gates of the Chaos! (Pistis Sophia, chapter 33)

Thus ends the story of the faithful Sophia. From the glorious Fullness she descended into alienation and chaos and was afflicted by the terrors of arrogance and ignorance. Having called out repeatedly in a mighty, magical voice to the Light, she was gifted with strength and sanctification from her bridegroom, Jesus, and led by his holy hand, she resumed her seat of wisdom in the kingdom of the mighty Aeons.

All archetypal myths possess a timeless quality that makes them applicable to the concerns of any place and time. The story of Sophia, in particular, fixes in comprehensible forms the universal elements that join psychic and transcendental experiences. Insights into the development (individuation) of the individual psyche, into sociological issues (including the elevation and emancipation of women in society), and into theological and metaphysical ideas can all be derived from the Sophianic myth.

The story of Sophia follows, with slight modifications, the classical four stages of ancient Greek drama, namely, *agone* or "contest," *pathos* or "defeat," *threnos* or "lamentation," and *theophania* or "the divinely accomplished solution" or "redemption." Consciousness is ever engaged in an aeonial contest with unconsciousness and suffers frequent defeat at the hands of its forces. Awareness of these defeats is crucial; hence the emphasis on lamentation, exemplified here by the many repentances of Sophia. Last is the joyous mystery of redemption, in which a divine redeemer comes from outside the existential milieu. In Greek theater this was the *deus ex machina*—an actor playing the role of the god was lowered onto the stage from above.

The predicament of the loss of wholeness, symbolized by Sophia's departure from the Fullness, is the ever-present predicament of all beings, most particularly humans. All of us are in desperate need of the restoration of our wholeness through union with our inmost self, the glory dwelling, though hidden, within us. Like Sophia, we wander over the face of the earth, our glory degraded and prostituted, while through the aeonic regions descends to meet us the "ever-coming One," our divine bridegroom, the Logos of the most high God. Thus the *theophania*, the divine resolution of the great drama, is ever here.

The Gnostics did not confine their vision to images of intrapsychic principles, as many contemporary depth psychologists do. For them the inner drama always mirrored the cosmic and indeed the transcosmic drama; as the story unfolded on high, so it is reflected and duplicated in the human soul. They regarded the Christ in us and the Sophia in us as our twin hopes of glory, seeking each other in holy longing and divine desire. The celestial pair, bearing these same names, were the supernal prototypes whose actions are repeated within the souls and spirits of men and women.

WHENCE COMETH SOPHIA?

Although the figure of Sophia, and the myth of her fall and redemption, were undoubtedly publicized and poetically expanded by the Gnostics, they were not the product of second- or third-century thought. The Old Testament contains numerous references to the wisdom of God as a feminine hypostasis (emanation) of God, existing before the creation of the world and mystically present in the visionary and intuitive experiences of prophets and sages. The Hebrew word for "wisdom" is *chokmah,* which during the Hellenistic period was translated into Greek as *sophia.* An entire body of biblical literature is named the "wisdom literature" and comprises such works as Proverbs, Ecclesiastes, Ecclesiasticus, the Book of the Wisdom, and the Song of Songs. Some of these books were declared apocryphal by the Protestant reformers, but they were highly regarded in many quarters, both Catholic and Protestant. In many of the Old Testament wisdom books, Chokmah-Sophia speaks to the reader in the first person, as in a revelatory discourse. She always appears as female and she regularly declares that she participated with God in early cosmic acts of creation. Here is an example from the Book of Proverbs (8.22–24, 27):

The Lord possessed me from the beginning of his way, before his
   works of old.
I was set up from everlasting, from the beginning, or ever the
   earth was.
When there were no depths I was brought forth. . . .
When he prepared the heavens I was there: when he set a compass
   upon the face of the depth.

She also introduces herself in exalted terms in Ecclesiasticus (24.5,
7–10, 14):

I came out of the mouth of the most High and covered the earth as a
cloud. I dwelt in high places, and my throne is a cloudy pillar. I alone
compassed the circuit of the sky and walked in the bottom of the deep;
in the waves of the sea and in all the earth and in every people and
nation. . . . He created me from the beginning, before the world and I
shall never fail.

The greatest Jewish theologian and philosopher to develop the
biblical teachings concerning Sophia was undoubtedly Philo of Alexandria, at times known as Philo the Jew. This outstanding religious
thinker, who was contemporaneous with very early Christianity (he
died about 50 A.D.), developed many teachings that are similar to those
of the Gnostics. Philo recognized the potential for divine knowledge
in humanity but also stated that to stimulate such knowledge certain
emanations of God must come into contact with humans. One of
these is the Logos, God's first-born outpouring, or "son"; another is
Sophia, the Wisdom of God, whom Philo calls the mother of all creation. This attribute of Sophia Philo derives from the statement in
Proverbs just quoted. Philo's orthodoxy within the Jewish context was
never challenged. Thus it seems that teachings such as his, especially
the ones concerning Sophia, were current in Jewish circles of his time
and were not considered heretical.

The specific Gnostic version of the myth of Sophia was probably enunciated first by the controversial and mysterious Simon Magus, who lived in the apostolic period and expounded a doctrine that has many affinities with the later elaborations of the myth of Sophia. Although he does not seem to have used the name *Sophia,* Simon taught concerning a divine female emanation who descended into the material world and was held captive there (for Simon's proto-Sophianic myth, see chapter 8). Present-day scholarship is inclined to view Sophia as Jewish in origin. In spite of the patriarchal monotheism espoused by mainstream Judaism, the presence of goddess figures is frequently indicated in Jewish history (as Raphael Patai has shown in his pioneering work, *The Hebrew Goddess*). Some of these feminine deities were undoubtedly chthonic fertility goddesses of Babylonian or related derivation who had little in common with Sophia. However, there may also have been a tradition concerning a more spiritual figure, the Wisdom of God, appearing in some cases as God's daughter and in others as his spouse. In the Hellenistic period, the religious climate among the Jews may also have softened to the point that the literature concerning this figure—as also philosophical pronouncements about her such as Philo's—could appear openly. The Gnostic teachers were then able to develop fully the story of Our Lady Wisdom.

It is no exaggeration to say that Sophia is present in virtually all Gnostic literature. The majority of the Nag Hammadi scriptures contain references to the Sophia myth, some explicit, others implicit. Of the scriptures that were available prior to the discovery of the Nag Hammadi library, the chief one is undoubtedly Pistis Sophia (Faithful Sophia), upon which the account of the fall and redemption of Sophia given earlier in this chapter is based. It is quite likely that a major part of the book was written by the great Gnostic teacher Valentinus, while additional passages may have been added by his disciples. It is the most complete account of the story of Sophia, surpassing in detail and poetic beauty all other works on the subject.

Pistis Sophia consists of three books of Jesus' discourses to his disciples, who are present with him on the Mount of Olives during the period between his resurrection and ascension. The first two concern the story of Sophia. Book 1 starts with a description of Jesus' spectacular transfigurative experience, in the course of which he ascends into the aeons in a blaze of light. After his return, he relates his discovery of Sophia in her fallen condition and tells how he prepared to assist her. In book 2, Jesus relates the reverses and intricacies of Sophia's ascent towards the Light and her restoration to her place in the thirteenth aeon. The discourses are delivered by Jesus in a formal, dramatic setting on the Mount of Olives Sophia's repentances are followed by recitations of psalms and passages from the Odes of Solomon, another Gnostic scripture. There are questions and discussions by the disciples, among whom Mary Magdalene occupies a prominent position.

Fig. 4. Gnostic gem, circa third century after Christ, depicting a many-armed Goddess figure. This figure holds various instruments of power in each hand and is surrounded by stars on all sides. There are two supernumerary heads of possible astrological significance. The figure may possibly represent the Gnostic Sophia.

The numerous Gnostic references to Sophia do not agree in every detail, although the main motif is identical in all. The cause of Sophia's fall is sometimes attributed to her presumption, sometimes to her loving desire for the Father, and in yet other texts to her desire to conceive by herself, without her male consort. Similarly, there are slight divergences in the interpretation of Sophia's relation to the Demiurge. Some accounts say that Sophia first brought forth the material elements of which the defective creation is made and then bore the Demiurge as the governor of this defective cosmos; others maintain that all of the flawed creation was the work of the Demiurge. In all these accounts, the figure of Sophia plays a crucial role in the fate of the universe and humanity.

WHAT BECAME OF SOPHIA?

The Sophia tradition reached its greatest flowering at the hands of the Gnostics, particularly in the school of Valentinus. After the suppression of Gnosticism in the third and fourth centuries, the Western Church subjected the figure of Sophia to deliberate neglect. The wisdom literature of the Old Testament was treated as if it referred to an abstract intellectual quality called wisdom, instead of to a personal divine being who is a hypostasis of the ultimate Godhead. The fact that, in addition to the wisdom literature, many other books of both the Old and the New Testaments contain references to Sophia was also conveniently ignored. (These include Genesis, Exodus, the Book of Job, the Gospels of Mark and John, many of St. Paul's letters—particularly 1 Corinthians and 1 Thessalonians—and the Revelation of St. John the Divine.) It is in the esoteric Judaism of the Kabbalah that one encounters a close approximation to Sophia in the greatly revered figure of the Shekinah, the feminine spiritual presence in the Sephira

Malkuth. Present-day scholars like the late and great Gershom Scholem have referred to the Kabbalists as Jewish Gnostics, and thus it is not surprising that the Gnostic Sophia found a home in their midst.

Roman Catholic Christendom experienced only one revival of the cult of Sophia. This came about in the twelfth century through the agency of St. Bernard of Clairvaux, the Cistercian abbot and mystic who wrote a lengthy mystical and poetic treatise based on the Song of Songs. Since the Roman Catholic Church had subsumed what was left of Sophia in the figure of the Virgin Mary, Bernard had a hard time distinguishing the mysterious Shulamite from the Madonna. His devotion to his vision of the figure of Sophia was nevertheless genuine and influential.

Sophia also made her appearance in alchemy. One of the great documents relating to the alchemical Sophia is the celebrated treatise *Aurora Consurgens,* attributed by many authorities to St. Thomas Aquinas, the noted medieval doctor of the church and father of Western theology. This outstanding work depicts the process of alchemical transformation as a gradual liberation of Sophia from her imprisonment in chaotic, confining materiality. Thereafter, it was not until the fresh spiritual and intellectual breezes of the Renaissance began to blow over Europe, building eventually to the revolutionary fervor of the Protestant Reformation, that the figure of Sophia appeared once more to the people of the West. The German mystic Jacob Boehme, a post-Reformation figure of major import in European religious thought, wrote insightfully about Sophia (see chapter 11).

Inspired in no small measure by Jacob Boehme and his interpreters, the alternative mystical and occult traditions of Western culture preserved the veneration of Sophia (often under her Latin name, Sapientia) through the centuries and thus made it available to future generations. Kabbalists (both Jewish and Christian); practitioners of high magic; and members of secret brotherhoods, such as the

Rosicrucians and esoteric Freemasons, frequently had affinity for Sophia.

One place where Sophia has been present since the early Christian centuries, albeit without much fanfare, is Eastern Orthodox Christianity. Orthodox theologians never abandoned the teaching that a feminine manifestation of God exists in the superterrestrial realm and inspires godly persons to wisdom. The cathedral of Hagia Sophia in Constantinople, once the greatest church in Christendom, was named in her honor, and many Greek and other Orthodox churches are dedicated to her even today. Sophiology (theology related to Sophia) received a monumental boost in the late nineteenth and early twentieth centuries largely through the work of Vladimir S. Soloviev, a Russian philosopher and poet who was deeply influenced by ancient Gnostic ideas. Born in 1853 and deceased just before World War I and the Bolshevik Revolution, Soloviev left a lasting mark on Russian spirituality. He was openly involved in the teachings of the Gnostics and wrote poems and essays with overtly Gnostic themes. Like a true Gnostic, Soloviev was no mere theoretician: he was a visionary and prophet, and the chief object of his gnosis was none other than Sophia. Three times—in 1862, in 1875, and at his death in 1900—he experienced encounters with Sophia. He was a great reviver of Russian Orthodox Sophiology, and his work was continued by other philosophers and theologians after his death.

Not surprisingly, the rise of feminist consciousness in the last part of the twentieth century has brought feminine divine figures into prominence, including Sophia. She has become one of the names that feminists and feminist sympathizers like to include in their pantheon of goddesses. Regrettably, many of these efforts are not informed via insight into the Gnostic scriptures, according to which, Sophia is a totally spiritual being, quite unrelated to the earth goddesses and lunar feminine deities of pagan religions. It might be fair to state that Sophia in any and all of her manifestations (ancient Gnostic, as Shulamite, as Shekinah, alchemical, Boehmean, Eastern Orthodox) has little in common with the sexualized and politicized images of "the goddess" as these appear in feminist and New Age sources.

The present renewed interest in mythology, folklore, and iconography, often including primitive and archaic images and legends, might be extended to include Sophia. Writers who tend to synthesize disparate images might mistakenly perceive Sophia in various mythological figures only because they are female. But gender was never an important or profound characteristic of mythological figures in general, nor of Gnostic figures in particular. Androgynous, genderless, and gender-changing features are frequent in the shape-shifting world of Gnostic mythic beings. Not all that glitters is gold; not all that is mythic and female is Sophia!

Today, as before, Sophia remains the great prototype of our exiled and alienated human condition. The term *alien* has taken on a new color in present-day culture. The pseudomythology of the television screen, based on science fiction, has defined *alien* for us as a usually menacing visitor from a distant planetary system. Even so, the image of the exile, or the alien, finds resonance in many minds and hearts. Not only is the phenomenon of exile prominently present in our world, but many who have never left the geography of their native land feel themselves as strangers not only in a strange land but in an alien world.

To the non-Gnostic, alienation might resemble a pathology; to the Gnostic, the consciousness of alienness is a valuable asset. As Sophia fell into dark chaos, so our consciousness has fallen into obscurity and forlornness. And as Sophia was in due course rescued by the Supreme Messenger, so we also shall be rescued in the fullness of our own time and restored to our own habitat in the aeons of truth and love.

THE GNOSTIC CHRIST:
SAVIOR OR LIBERATOR?

At the beginning of the twenty-first century, we readily encounter a bewildering number of characterizations of Jesus. In the world of popular entertainment, the legacy of the 1960s included *Jesus Christ Superstar*, where Jesus appears as a somewhat eccentric social critic. In the perilous sphere of politics, we find the liberation theologians, who do their best to portray Jesus as a proto-Marxist revolutionary, a sort of first-century Che Gueverra. In the more sober world of scholarship, we find the rather dull Jesus of the Jesus Seminar and of the conjectured "Q document." To these we might add the phallic-psychedelic Jesus presented by the eccentric Dead Sea Scrolls scholar John Allegro, or the scheming Jesus extolled by Allegro's colleague Hugh Schonfield. The revolutionary Jesus, the sensuous Jesus—so many Jesuses and so little clarity! In the last quarter of the twentieth century we were introduced to them all. All of these images of Jesus, and quite a few more, are based on the New Testament. It has been pointed out more than once that on the basis of this evidence the central figure of

Fig. 5. Anthropomorphic crosses of the Cathars. The human shape of the cross as well as the T-shaped cross surmounted by the circle symbolize the heavenly man, or Christ.

Christianity can be made out to be almost anything anyone wants him to be. Ever since the introduction of the rationalistic approach to the Bible in the form of higher biblical criticism and similar approaches, the search for the "historical Jesus" has been on, yet in more than one way this search seems to have failed.

Neglected, however, is perhaps the most influential Jesus of early Christendom: the Gnostic Jesus. To the early Christians, Jesus was not so much a historical figure as an inspiration. Witness, for instance, Paul the Apostle's description of Jesus as "far above all rule and authority, and power and dominion, and above every name that is named, not only in this age [*aeon*] but in that which is to come" (Eph. 1.21). This statement is so Gnostic in tone that one might conclude that Paul and others did view Jesus in Gnostic terms—as a being superior to the authorities and their kin (the Demiurge and the archons) of this lower world.

For a long time, the only sources for the teachings of Jesus were the four Gospels. Of these, the Gospel of John has always been the favorite of Gnostics and of Gnosticizing esotericists throughout history. Along with miracle stories and an account of the passion, death, and resurrection, the Gospel of John includes a number of discourses attributed to Jesus that have a great deal in common with the teachings in distinctly Gnostic literature.

The Gospel of John is not the only canonical evidence for the Gnostic character of the teachings of Jesus. At least part of the considerable body of the sayings of Jesus was incorporated into the Gospels of Matthew and Luke, and some even into Mark. Many of the sayings in the canonical gospels contain teachings that make eminent sense when interpreted in a Gnostic light. A good example is the parable of the wheat and tares in Mark (13.24–30): A man sows good wheat seed in his field, but later finds that an enemy has sown weeds among the wheat. When the workers ask if they should pull the weeds out, the farmer tells them to allow both wheat and weeds to grow until the time of the harvest, when the two can be more easily separated. According to Gnostic teaching, the world is a mixture of the seeds of light and of darkness. Though it is impossible to distinguish between them now, in the fullness of time they will separate naturally, as ordained.

JESUS AS GNOSTIC TEACHER

There are many sayings attributed to Jesus that are not found in the canonical Gospels but are included in Gnostic scriptures. The greatest profusion of these is in the Gospel according to Thomas, which is part of the Nag Hammadi collection. The Gnostic scribes seem to have been principally interested in recording the teachings of Jesus characterized as secret—meaning the teachings of strictly Gnostic character that he gave to select disciples after his resurrection.

How did the Gnostics view Jesus? There is little doubt that they revered him exceedingly, that they saw in him a manifestation of the highest Godhead, and that they regarded him as the liberator and

enlightener who burst open the prison of humanity's confinement in material and mental unconsciousness. According to the Gnostic tradition, Jesus exercised his ministry in two principal ways. The first of these might be called his ministry of teaching. The second was a sacramental ministry of initiatory and liberating mysteries (see chapter 7). It is quite likely that the common people in Palestine regarded him primarily as a rabbi or lay teacher of religion, since he did not belong to the hereditary priestly caste. Thus, in a sense, the role of teacher was his external persona, while that of spiritual hierophant was more hidden.

Fig. 6. Cathar gravestone, shaped roughly in the likeness of a man's head and trunk. It also shows the symbol of the encircled, equal-armed cross, indicating balance.

The majority of the sayings of Jesus contained in the Gospel according to Thomas can be classified under four headings: (1) sayings concerning the human condition; (2) sayings regarding human conduct; (3) sayings alluding to his own role as redeemer or liberator; and (4) sayings emphasizing the importance of self-knowledge as a precondition for the knowledge of the Divine. In all of these sayings, the reader is struck by what might be called an existential attitude of great practicality evinced by Jesus. He repeatedly refuses to be drawn into theoretical discussions regarding the relationship of spirit and body, the exact time of his reappearance on earth, the necessity of following the commandments instituted by Moses, or even the exact character of his own messianic role. Instead, he most often reminds his listeners of the harm done by their anxieties, their dogmatic fixations, and their attachments to earthly things as well as their psychological foibles. In quite a few instances, he seems to be saying: Don't be weighed down by obsessive concerns for your material welfare or even for your moral character. Proceed on your journey from limitation and attachments to the greater life that awaits you. It matters little whether you are circumcised or not, or what diet you observe. It matters less whether you think that I am Elijah returned or a philosopher or a mere carpenter's son. What matters is whether you make sincere efforts to know yourselves and thus be prepared for liberating gnosis. His message is well-characterized by the shortest saying in this gospel: "Be passers by" (saying 42). (A detailed exposition of some of the sayings in the Gospel according to Thomas, is in Hoeller, *Jung and the Lost Gospels.*)

The Gnostic sayings of Jesus also shed light on his rather unusual method of teaching. Unlike most teachers, he appears to impart more than ideas, to do more than exhort along conventional moral and religious lines. He addresses his teaching not to the thinking minds and the emotions of people as much as to their incipient intuitive gnosis. His words are not so much intended to inform as to stimulate latent creative and imaginative faculties. The Jesus who emerges in these sayings is a Jesus quite different from the traditional meek and mild man of sorrows. This Jesus uses metaphor and myth, cryptic mystical adages and explicitly Gnostic parables, to induce extraordinary states of consciousness in his followers.

A number of sayings in the Gospel according to Thomas show Jesus as a teacher intent upon stimulating gnosis in his followers. He rebukes the disciples for trying to assess his role and person in terms of past prophecies:

His disciples said to him: "Twenty-four prophets spoke in Israel and they all spoke about Thee." He said to them: "You have dismissed the living one who is before you, and you have spoken about the dead." (saying 52)

He seems to be saying: Don't evaluate me in terms of the past; don't connect me with prophecy, scripture, and expectation. See me with your gnosis and you will understand. In the same source we find:

Look upon the living one as long as you live, lest you die and seek to see him and be unable to see. (saying 59)

And:

They said to him: "Tell us who thou art so we may believe in thee." He said: "You test the face of the sky and of the earth, but him who is before your face you have not known and you do not know how to test this moment." (saying 91)

All of these statements appeal to an immediate intuitive perception of an existential nature and discard conceptual, intellectual explanations.

The Gnostic scriptures reveal that at least in some instances Jesus actually induced the experience of gnosis in his followers. In saying 13 of the Gospel according to Thomas, Jesus asks his disciples to tell him whom he resembles. Peter likens his master to a righteous angel; Matthew likens him to a wise philosopher. Only Thomas refuses to make any comparison and says that his mouth cannot declare in any way what his master is like. Jesus then says to Thomas:

I am not thy master [any longer], because thou hast drunk, thou hast become inebriated by the bubbling spring which I have measured out.

Jesus then takes Thomas aside and whispers three words into his ear. Afterwards, the other apostles try to learn from Thomas what the three words are. Thomas refuses to tell them, saying:

> If I tell you one of the words which he said to me, you will take up stones and throw them at me; and fire will come from the stones and burn you up.

There is a more mundane version of this incident, omitting the role of Thomas, in the Gospel of Matthew (16.13).

Thomas had become "inebriated," that is, he had experienced a nonordinary state of consciousness, and in this state he had known Jesus through gnosis. To disclose his gnosis to those who had not experienced that depth would have been a fatal mistake. The sad fate of numerous Gnostics throughout history bears testimony to the blind fury that the nonknower may vent on the knower.

ATONEMENT OR LIBERATION?

The dominant contemporary Christian belief is that Jesus came to atone for the sins of humankind and thus make salvation possible. The justification for this belief is, in brief: God created a good world, which became a fallen world due to God's wrath once the first humans disobeyed God. Death and suffering were introduced into what, until then, had been a paradisiacal creation. In time, God's wrath waned and he sought to reconcile himself to humankind again. The agent of this reconciliation was God's only begotten son, Jesus Christ, who was sent by his Father into the world to suffer and to die on the cross for the sins of humanity, including the original sin committed by the ancestors of the human race.

The postulates of this "atonement theology" have come under

question as the result of the scientific discoveries of the last two centuries. If death was brought into the world by human sin, how is it that so many life forms perished long before human life appeared on earth? Life was preying upon life long before men and women joined the fray. Perhaps the original creation was not as benign and paradisiacal as we have thought. Perhaps the world has always been what has aptly been called a giant predatory cafeteria, and humans merely became part of the food chain at a relatively late period.

The Gnostic followers of Christ, quite early in the history of the Christian faith, refused to go along with the atonement theology. Even without the evidence of biology and paleontology, they did not accept the notion that a good world had been corrupted by evil humans and then had to be reconciled to a wrathful God by the torment and death of Jesus. Does this mean that Gnostics did not regard Jesus as their redeemer? Far from it. As we saw earlier, the Gnostics felt that they were strangers on this earth, indeed in this cosmos. One of their teachers, Marcion, calls this world *haec cellula creatoris,* meaning "this prison cell made by the Creator." The Mandaean Gnostic scripture, the Ginza, admonishes human beings: "Thou wert not from here, and thy root was not of this world." The redeemer came not to pacify his angry Father by dying in ignominy, but rather to "take captivity captive" (as a Gnostic phrase expressed it) and liberate the forlorn strangers from the prison cell where they found themselves.

People only superficially acquainted with Gnosticism often conclude that to the Gnostic, salvation or liberation is an unmediated experience, requiring no savior. Nothing could be farther from the truth. The human spirit, say the Gnostics, came into this world from outside it, and thus the stimulus for liberation must also come from outside. True, the liberating spiritual potential resides in the depths (or perhaps better, the heights) of the human soul itself, but realization of this potential requires powerful intervention. This assistance is rendered by beings whom certain schools of Gnosticism call messengers of Light—salvific, messianic figures sent by the highest Godhead. The great Gnostic prophet Mani of Persia states this clearly (as quoted by Al Biruni):

> Wisdom and good deeds have always from time to time been brought to mankind by the messengers of God. So in one age they have been brought by the messenger called Buddha to India, in another by Zarathustra to Iran, yet in another by Jesus to the West. Thereupon this revelation has come down, this prophecy in this latter age through me, Mani, the apostle of the God of truth in Babylonia. (Al Biruni, *Athar ul Bakiya*)

Without naming the name of the messenger, the Ginza tells it well:

> In the name of him who came, in the name of him who comes, and in the name of him who is brought forth. In the name of the Great Stranger who has fought his way through the worlds, who came, split the firmament, and revealed himself. (chapter 35)

In Christian Gnosticism, this great stranger is Jesus. In many scriptures of the Gnostic tradition he is called the *Logos;* in others, the *Soter* (healer, savior); and in many, the *Christos* (anointed one). The exact relationship of these names to each other is not always clear. There are indications that the Gnostics believed that the spiritual Christ descended into the person of Jesus at the time of his baptism in the river Jordan at the hands of John. Yet Jesus was also regarded as a holy and supernal being from birth.

To sum up, salvation to the Gnostic means not reconciliation with an angry God by way of the death of his son, but rather liberation from the stupor induced by earthly existence and an awakening by way of gnosis. Gnostics do not hold that any kind of sin, including that of Adam and Eve, is powerful enough to cause the degradation of the entire manifest world. The world is flawed because that is its nature, but humans can become free from confinement in this flawed world and from the unconsciousness that accompanies this confinement. Jesus came as a messenger and liberator, and those who take his message to heart and participate in his mysteries are, like the disciple Thomas, saved by gnosis.

RESURRECTION OR AWAKENING?

One of the most portentous accusations voiced against Gnostics by the orthodox is that they rejected the resurrection of Jesus. In fact, there is no evidence that the Gnostics denied the resurrection. They did say, however, that the resurrection, like most events recounted in the New Testament, is not to be taken literally. Some sort of reanimation of Jesus' body may have taken place on Easter morning. In fact, in most Gnostic scriptures the post-resurrection Jesus is referred to as the "living one," an equivalent of the Latin *redivivus,* "one who has returned to life," but this does not mean that Jesus came back to life in a physical body like ours. Indeed, there was doubt whether he ever occupied a physical body like ours. Physical bodies do not walk on water, pass through walls, or shine like the sun. The precise nature of Jesus' body is a mystery, said the Gnostics, and they felt this applied to both the body he occupied before the resurrection and the one in which he appeared thereafter.

In fact, the canonical Gospels are uncertain regarding the precise nature of the "resurrection body" occupied by Jesus. Certainly some Gospel accounts suggest that it was solid and composed of flesh; however, others leave room for doubt. The story of the road to Emmaus, recounted in both Luke and Mark, states that Jesus appeared "in another form" (Mark 1.12; Luke 24.13–32), and that after he blessed the bread at the table he simply vanished into thin air. In the Gospel of

John (20.11–17), Mary Magdalene, who surely was well acquainted with her master's appearance, encounters him near the grave and mistakes him for the gardener. After she recognizes him, he instructs her not to touch him. This command, the celebrated *noli me tangere* (do not touch me), which gave rise to so much sacred art, can certainly be interpreted as indicating that his body was insubstantial. Elaine Pagels, in her book *The Gnostic Gospels* (6), states: "So if some of the New Testament stories insist on a literal view of the resurrection, others lend themselves to different interpretations."

Which was more important about Jesus, his fleshly body or his spirit? Even the most orthodox might answer that it was his spirit. It is quite understandable, therefore, that the Gnostics emphasized the spiritual nature of Jesus and his resurrection. The two views agreed that, both before and after the resurrection, Jesus *appeared* to be occupying a body of flesh. Many Gnostics felt that this body itself might be an appearance *(doketos)*, and thus they were accused of being docetists, that is, those who think that Jesus' body was purely illusionary. (However, the concept of an "appearance body" is well known elsewhere—in the traditions of India, for instance.)

More important for the Gnostics than the substance of Jesus' body is the Gnostic teaching that the resurrection has a deeply personal spiritual meaning for everyone who aspires to gnosis. For are we not all, in a certain sense, dead and entombed in material darkness, wrapped in the winding sheet of unconsciousness? Is our vision not obstructed by a stone of obscurity and obtuseness? And is it not our dearest hope and glorious destiny to see that stone rolled away and our spiritual nature awakened from its aeonial slumber? If this is so, then why not do as Christ did and resurrect into a new life of the spirit? Quite so, say the orthodox, but this will happen only after our death, when on Judgment Day the long-decayed and long-vanished flesh of our bodies will rise again. It is here that the Gnostic unequivocally parts company with the orthodox. The Gnostic is likely to quote from the Gospel of Philip: "First Christ rose and then he died"—and he might add that if we wish to engage in the imitation of Christ, this is what we, too, must do. For as the same gospel states elsewhere:

> If men do not first experience the resurrection while they are alive, they will not receive anything when they die. (saying 21)

The Gnostics regarded the term *resurrection* as a word-symbol for gnosis, or true spiritual awakening. When we awaken to the consciousness of who we are, where we come from, and where we are going, we have arrived at knowledge of the things that truly are. To the Gnostic tradition, Christ's resurrection is the mysterious inducement facilitating our own resurrection or awakening. If this awakening does not take place, then Christ's life, death, resurrection, and ascension were in vain. As Angelus Silesius, the seventeenth-century Christian mystic, who was more than a little bit Gnostic, wrote:

> Though Christ a thousand times in Bethlehem be born,
> And not in thee, thy soul is all forlorn.
> The cross at Golgatha standeth up in vain,
> Unless in thee it be erect again.
>
> *(The Cherubic Wanderer)*

The *imitatio Christi* (imitation of Christ) has often been understood as identification of one's own misfortunes and sufferings with those in the passion and crucifixion. However, this imitation must also include the resurrection. The Gnostic position is rather clear: In the moment of full gnosis the indwelling divine spark is effectively released and one rises up from the double sepulchre of body and mind, united with the timeless spirit. Forgetfulness falls away; remembrance of the realities of the spirit returns.

CHRIST THE TIMELESS LIBERATOR

One of the chief Muslim objections to the Christian view of Jesus is that he is called the son of God. In Muslim eyes, it is unbecoming to say that God might have a son, for procreation is an activity of the flesh and thus beneath the dignity of divinity. While the Gnostic scriptures freely refer to Father, Son, and Holy Spirit, they do not equate Jesus with the second person of the Trinity in any explicit fashion. The issue of sonship was not important to them. Like the Muslims, they might even have shied away from it. Jesus the anointed *(Christos)*, to them, was a mysterious aeonial being, a great spiritual power that descended in the form of a messenger to humanity. The Mandaean Ginza (389 ff.) presents the self-disclosure of just such a being, although his name is not mentioned:

> From the place of light have I gone forth,
> from thee, bright habitation.
> I come to feel the hearts,
> to measure and try all minds,
> to see in whose heart I dwell,
> in whose mind I repose.
> Who thinks of me, of him I think;
> who calls my name, his name I call.
> Who prays my prayer from down below,
> his prayer I pray from the place of light.
> I came and found the truthful and believing hearts.
> When I was not dwelling among them,
> yet my name was on their lips.
> I took them and guided them up to the world of light.

The church father Hippolytus gives us a statement of the Gnostic savior as preserved by a Gnostic school called the Peratae: "I am the voice of awakening in the Aeon of the eternal night." In the Naasene "Psalm of the Soul" we find the heavenly, spiritual Christ imploring the Father to send him to accomplish his redemptive mission:

> For the sake of humanity send me, Father! Holding the seals will I descend, through all the Aeons will I take my way, all the Mysteries will I unlock, the forms of the divine beings I will make manifest, the secrets of the sacred Way, known as Gnosis, I will transmit.

Jesus bears testimony to his own high and mysterious station in a number of sayings of the Gospel according to Thomas. To cite a few:

> I have cast fire upon the world, and see I guard it, until the world is afire. (saying 10)

> I will give you what eye has not seen and what ear has not heard and what hand has not touched and what has not arisen in the heart of men. (saying 17)

> Whoever drinks from my mouth shall become as I am and I myself will become he, and the hidden things shall be revealed to him. (saying 108)

> Whoever is near to me is near to the fire, and whoever is far from me is far from the kingdom. (saying 82)

> I am the light that is above them all, I am the all, the all came forth from me, and the all attained to me. Cleave the wood, I am there; lift up the stone and you will find me there. (saying 77)

The Gnostic Jesus Christ is truly much more than the carpenter's son from Nazareth. In certain ways he is also more than the precisely defined and described son of God of the theologians. If the Gnostic Jesus appears as a paradox and an enigma to some, it is because the Gnostic perception of Jesus originates in the experience of gnosis. The Gnostics saw Jesus with visionary eyes. To them he was a transcendental being, a denizen of another dimension or realm who had temporarily found himself on earth. To know Jesus, one had to receive gnosis.

Then his words, his actions, his very being would be revealed and understood entirely. Today, after fully two thousand years of Christian history, the great messianic enigma still calls to us and asks us to understand him with a mind and perception of gnosis. About those who view him with prosaic eyes he still says:

> I seem to them like a stranger because I am from another race. (Odes of Solomon 41)

To the Gnostic, however, he will forever be the luminous stranger who reminds us that we also are from another world to which he can help us to return.

THE MYSTERY OF INIQUITY:
THE GNOSTIC VIEW OF EVIL

On June 10, 1991, a cover story appeared in *Time* magazine on the topic of evil. The author, Lance Morrow, did not argue for a particular thesis and did not reach any conclusions. What he did, however, was in a sense more important. He began by stating three propositions:

- God is all-powerful.
- God is all-good.
- Terrible things happen.

Citing several sources, Morrow said that one could agree with any two of these propositions, but not all three. You can declare that there is an all-powerful God who allows terrible things to happen, but this God could not be all-good. On the other hand, there might be an all-good God who lets terrible things happen because he does not have the power to stop them; thus he is not all-powerful.

This analysis might easily have been given by a Gnostic of the first three or four centuries of the Christian era, or for that matter by a contemporary Gnostic, such as the present writer. Not that Gnostics were the only ones who recognized this uniquely monotheistic predicament. The supreme luminary of medieval Catholic theology, St. Thomas Aquinas, admitted in his *Summa Theologica* that the existence of evil is the best argument against the existence of God. If the concept of a monotheistic God is accepted, then evil has no viable explanation. Conversely, if evil exists, then the monotheistic God presented by the mainstream religious traditions of the West cannot exist.

WHENCE COMETH EVIL?

Religious traditions throughout history have accounted for the existence of evil in a number of ways. The first is monistic; the second is radically dualistic; the third relates evil to ignorance; while the fourth attributes evil to original sin. In primeval times, the undifferentiated nature of human consciousness allowed people to say that both good and bad come from the Divine. Thus archaic shamans would not have found it difficult to say that good and evil are visited upon human beings by the Great Spirit. In the more sophisticated context of the Sumero-Babylonian traditions, it was believed that the gods amused themselves by creating terrible things: freakish beings, evil demons, and horrible conditions for human life.

To employ a psychohistorical rationale—as elsewhere throughout this analysis—one might say that before human beings had developed a differentiated consciousness (or conscious ego), they easily envisioned God or the gods as like themselves, so that the coincidence of good and evil was part of their, as well as the gods', nature. More advanced spiritual traditions have inherited some of this monistic attitude; thus mystical Jewish theology says that God partakes of both good and evil tendencies (*yetzirim*).

With the development of consciousness, the mind begins to differentiate between the beneficent and the malefic sides of being. The tension of trying to hold a concept of God that unites good and evil becomes unbearable, so that the mind must separate the two. The notion of radical dualism thus arises, for which the most prominent example is Zoroastrianism. Here the true and good God, Ahura Mazda (sometimes called Ormazd), has a divine antagonist known as Angra Mainyu (Ahriman). The two are engaged in a perennial cosmic struggle for supremacy. Although Ahura Mazda is supreme and his ultimate victory is assured, as long as creation endures Angra Mainyu will continue to fight him and bring suffering into the world.

A sophisticated but impersonal view of evil and its origins can be found in the great religions originating in India. These traditions view evil as part of the unenlightened state of existence and see the cause of evil as ignorance (*avidya*). By attaining enlightened consciousness and thus rising above all dualities, one is liberated from karma and from all conditions in which evil plays a role. Whether liberation inevitably leads to the cessation of incarnate existence is not always clear, but life as one has known it clearly ceases, and with it evil ceases also.

The fourth category comprises classical monotheism as it is found in mainstream Judaism and Christianity. While the traditions of the other three categories ascribe the existence of evil to God, to a malign counter-God, or to human ignorance, Judeo-Christian thought assigns the origin of evil to human sin. As we saw in chapter 3, the creation myth of the mainstream Judeo-Christian tradition, with its story of the Garden of Eden and the curious events said to have transpired there, forms the foundation for this view. That is, the transgressions committed by the first human pair brought about the "fall" of creation, resulting in the present state of the world.

Even in a secularized age like our own, the powerful shadow of such beliefs continues to cast a pall on our minds. One wonders how differently history would have proceeded had the guilt of the Fall not been present to oppress the souls of men and women in Judeo-Christian culture!

THE GNOSTIC VIEW

Gnostics, both ancient and modern, agree with the Buddhists that suffering is the existential manifestation of evil in the world. Although the suffering of humans, with their complex physiology and psychology, is of a singularly refined nature, all other creatures also experience fear, pain, and misery. As St. Paul points out, all creation groans and travails in pain (Rom. 8.22). As noted in chapter 2, the Gnostics see this imperfect state of the world as the result, not of original sin, but of an original flaw. Put in slightly more abstract terms, evil is part of the fabric of the world we live in. If there is a Creator of this reality, then surely this Creator is responsible for the evil in it. For believers in monotheistic religions, however, the Gnostic position appears blasphemous, and even those who consider themselves unbelievers often view it with dismay.

The Gnostic position may best be understood in the light of its historical roots. According to most contemporary scholars, and as noted earlier, Gnosticism originated in the Jewish religious matrix (probably in its heterodox manifestations) and then came to ally itself with the Jewish heresy that became Christianity. As stated in chapter 2, the Gnostics were confronted with the image of a monotheistic God in the Old Testament—and adaptations of that image in the New Testament—who was often capricious, wrathful, vengeful, and unjust. It was easy to conclude that this apparently flawed God created a world in his own flawed image. The Gnostics asked the great question: Is this flawed Creator truly the ultimate, true, and good God, or is he a lesser deity who is either ignorant of a power beyond himself or is conscious of a divine authority superior to himself but decides to usurp the position of the highest Deity? The Gnostics answered that this Creator is obviously not the true, ultimate God but is rather a *demiurgos,* a secondary deity. The Demiurge is the originator of evil and imperfection in the world.

Thus the apparent blasphemy of attributing the world's evil to the Creator is revealed as originating in the Gnostics' confrontation with a monotheistic God. Hermeticism, a kindred movement to Gnosticism, is rooted in paganism. Because of these origins, the Hermeticists did not inherit and have to answer to the ambivalent figure of the Old Testament God, so they were able to adopt a less harsh position. Their concept of evil did not emphasize the relation of evil to the Demiurge. Today many people tend to favor Hermeticism over Gnosticism for this very reason.

Many have tried to avoid recognizing the flaws in this creation and therefore the flaws in its Creator, but none of their arguments have impressed the Gnostics. The ancient Greeks, especially the Neoplatonists, focused on the harmony of the universe, so that by venerating its grandeur they might forget their own afflictions, as well as the challenges and sorrows of ordinary life. Look at this beautiful world, they said; see the superb order in which it functions and perpetuates itself. How can one call something so beautiful and harmonious an evil thing? The Gnostics have always answered that the flaws, the forlornness, and the alienation of existence cannot be denied, so the universe is only partially harmonious and orderly.

To those influenced by Eastern spirituality, who argue that the law of karma—whereby one's misdeeds generate misfortune later in life or even in another life—explains the imperfection of the manifest world, the Gnostic might counter that karma can at best only explain how the chain of suffering and imperfection works. It does not tell us why such a sorrowful system should exist in the first place.

QUALIFIED DUALISM

As already mentioned, one way of explaining the existence of evil is radical dualism, of which the Zoroastrian faith is an example. The Gnostic position, by contrast, might be called qualified dualism. This position does not postulate warfare between a good deity and an evil deity, as does radical dualism. To state this view simply, good and evil are mixed in the manifest world; the world is not wholly evil, but it is not wholly good either. The evil in the world should not blind us to the presence of good; nor should the good blind us to the reality of evil.

The Gnostics themselves favored mythology as a means to express profound insights. There are myths telling of the commingling of good and evil in creation that predate the Gnostics. One of these tales is the Greek myth of Dionysus. When this god was torn apart by the Titans, Zeus came to his aid and blasted his attackers with a thunderbolt. The bodies of both the Titans and Dionysus were reduced to ashes and mixed. From these ashes rose all sorts of creatures, including humans, in which the divine nature of Dionysus was mingled with the evil nature of the Titans. Thus light and darkness are at war with each other within human nature and in the natural world.

The Gnostics had their own myth about the origins of good and evil. It begins with a boundless, blissful Fullness—the Pleroma—that is beyond all manifest existence. The Pleroma is both the abode of and the essential nature of the True Ultimate God *(alethes theos)*. Before time and before memory, this ineffable Fullness extended itself into the lower regions of being. In the course of this emanation, it manifested itself in a number of intermediate deities, *demiurgoi,* who were rather like great angels, endowed with enormous talents of creativity and organization. Some of these beings, however, became alienated from their supernal source and so took on evil tendencies. They created a physical world long before the creation of humans, and they created it in the likeness of their own imperfect natures.

Thus the will that created the world was tainted with self-will, arrogance, and the hunger for power; through the works performed by these alienated beings, evil came to penetrate creation. Ever since then, as the Gnostic teacher Basilides reportedly said, "Evil adheres to created existence as rust adheres to iron." As part of the creation, human beings also reflect the flawed nature of the creators. The human body is subject to disease, death, and other evils; even the soul *(psyche)* is not free from imperfection. Only the spirit *(pneuma),* hidden deep within the human essence, remains free from the evil and tends toward the True God.

CONTEMPORARY CONCLUSIONS

Terrible things do happen, as the *Time* essay stated, and as the history of the twentieth and early twenty-first centuries shows. The world contains evil and horror, and suffering is universal. Some individuals, often in powerful positions, torment and kill others on a daily basis. Believers in the Judeo-Christian monotheistic God and proponents of the karma theory may say that this does not matter all that much, because in the final analysis even evil leads to good. They seem to be saying that evil is not really evil at all, but good masquerading in an unpleasant disguise. This kind of topsy-turvy argument is an affront to all those who have looked evil in the face—survivors of the

Holocaust or the Gulag or the killing fields. For them, evil is evil, and all other explanations are but evasions.

Moreover, many terrible things happen that are not caused by human beings, such as earthquakes, fires, floods, and plagues. While the perversities of the human condition are responsible for some of the suffering in this world, much of it is not our fault. Frequently, however, we believe that it is. Yet, whether occasioned by the myth of Adam and Eve or by the propaganda that makes humans out to be the sole destroyers of the environment, the cultivation of guilt is no remedy for evil. On the contrary, guilt begets more sorrow in the long run. Let us be done with this self-flagellation and try to mitigate the evils over which we have some control, remembering that it is beyond our powers to eradicate misfortune altogether.

Since humans are made of the same stuff as the creation, it is as impossible to exorcise evil from ourselves entirely as it is to get rid of it in the world around us. If human schemes and techniques could eliminate evil from human nature, we would have succeeded at it long ago.

The myth of evil, the *mysterium iniquitatis,* presented by the Gnostics answers some questions while it raises others. Contemporary society is increasingly dominated by a certain secular bias that has its roots in eighteenth-century Enlightenment philosophy, while its trunk derives from Marxism, and its branches are largely made up of consumerism and hedonism—the worship of money, health, and youthfulness. This bias is founded on the assumption—sometimes tacit, sometimes overt—that only the tangible, physical world exists and that the supernatural is but a metaphor constellated around the physical. It is no wonder that powerful objections are raised against the Gnostic view.

Gnosticism in no way endorses our era's striving for a secular salvation, substituting theories of social mechanics for liberating gnosis. In the Gnostic view, neither human society nor the natural world is salvific, because the reality of both is derivative rather than primary. Nikolay Berdyaev, a modern philosopher with many Gnostic affinities, expressed this cogently: "The natural world, society, the state, the nation and the rest are partial, and their claim to totality is an enslaving lie, which is born of the idolatry of men."

The modern and postmodern myopia, which reduces the human to a highly intelligent but perverse animal and deifies both social and ecological engineering, is inimical to the Gnostic point of view. When this myopia predominates, life becomes horizontal. Everything that matters is right here and now—and is material, to boot. When the only evils are the depletion of the ozone layer and the overpopulation of the earth, then Gnostic considerations of evil and freedom from evil become mere shimmering mirages. Whatever one's opinion of the Gnostic myth of evil may be, its foundations are supernatural and spiritual, rather than naturalistic, sociological, or economic. The origin of evil is, in the words of St. Paul, "spiritual wickedness in high places"; therefore material means will not avail against it. This does not mean, of course, that evil material conditions should not be combated through whatever means are available, including material ones. To think, however, that any physical means will ever completely eliminate all evils and suffering is folly.

Gnostics have always been convinced that human beings are in fact spirits temporarily inhabiting a physical body in this physical world. Owing to the indwelling spirit *(pneuma)* deeply encased within our physical and psychic selves, we are capable of responding to the divine love coming to us from beyond the flawed system where we find ourselves. It is this love that offers us the opportunity for transcendental gnosis. In our contemporary milieu we often use the word *transcendental* but fail to realize that it means transcending the natural world, indeed the cosmos itself. Transcend is what we are intended to do. When we transcend the world, we transcend evil. Until then, the best we can do is exercise our powers of discernment to separate the good from the evil, the light from the darkness. In this way we work out our preliminary salvation in this world and become ready for our final salvation by gnosis.

Contemporary Gnostics for the most part agree with the fundamental insights of their ancient counterparts. Do modern Gnostics believe in the Demiurge? Do they believe that evil was planted in the world by the Demiurge? Do they regard these ideas as metaphysical truths or as mythologems hinting at more subtle and mysterious realities? Not surprisingly, some Gnostics believe these things literally, others believe them symbolically; still others hold a mixture of both views. What matters is not the precise form of these teachings but their substance. And this is clear enough. The Gnostic teachings speak of the reality and power of evil and its fundamental presence throughout manifest existence. They declare that while we may not be able to rid the world or ourselves of evil, we may, and indeed will, rise above it through gnosis. And when this extrication is accomplished, we shall indeed no longer fear the noonday devil or the terror that walks by night.

CHAPTER SEVEN

LIBERATING MYSTERIES:
GNOSTIC INITIATORY SACRAMENTS

When dealing with the ritual aspect of any spiritual tradition, we must first of all divorce ourselves from certain rationalistic notions that dominated the intellectual world in the nineteenth and early twentieth centuries and are not without adherents even today. The pet theory of the rationalistic schools of comparative religion says that the higher forms of religious traditions originated in philosophy and ethics and devolved later into systems of worship, eventually degenerating into ritual and magic. Basic to this idea is the view that philosophy and ethics are more advanced and nobler products of the human spirit than ceremony because the former originate in reason, while the latter is irrational in character.

This attitude has been the cause of much misunderstanding about Gnosticism. For many centuries, Gnosticism was thought to be primarily a product of philosophical speculation with little or no relationship to authentic religion or to the practical tasks of living. The Gnostics were represented as speculative philosophers and metaphysical dreamers who conjured up fantastic cosmological and theogonic systems and bemoaned the evils of the created world, while proclaiming that the task of the human spirit is to return to a never-never land beyond this world. Fortunately, the tide of scholarly opinion has now turned, and the nature of Gnostic views is becoming better understood, thanks to the labors of a more fair-minded generation of scholars and writers. This new attitude toward Gnosticism is well exemplified in the following statement by the noted European scholar Gilles Quispel, one of the principal translators of the famed Nag Hammadi texts:

> In my *Gnosis als Weltreligion* (1951) I suggested that Gnosticism expressed a specific religious experience, which was frequently turned into a myth. . . . It seems clear that at least some of the major Gnostic systems were inspired by vivid emotions and personal experience. And it is now generally accepted that Gnosticism was not a philosophy, or even a Christian heresy, but a religion with its own specific views about God, the world, and man. ("Gnosticism," in Cavendish, *Man, Myth, and Magic* 1115)

And, we might add, Gnosticism is a religion replete with sacraments that liberate the soul.

TALISMANS AND SACRAMENTS

It is indeed curious that certain truths regarding Gnosticism have not emerged until now, for quite early in the history of the study of Gnosticism there was much evidence that the Gnostics did more than speculate and philosophize. Gnostic books of ancient origin were, and are still being, discovered that are not of a philosophical nature but contain long prayers and invocations addressed to various transcendental powers. Incomprehensible words of power, consisting of long sequences of vowels, apparently designed for chanting, are found in many Gnostic texts. Moreover, numerous Gnostic scriptures contain lengthy records of rituals performed by Jesus, while others allude to well-developed sacramental systems within the Gnostic communities of the early centuries of the Christian era. Many Gnostic talismanic gems have also been discovered, all of which contain archetypal imagery: serpents, lions, astrological symbols, and hybrid mythological beings—like the celebrated ABRAXAS (or ABRASAX), which has the head of a rooster, the body of a man, and legs fashioned like snakes. Very likely viewed as incomprehensible and even reprehensible by the rationalistic mind, this wealth of symbolic and ritualistic literature was largely allowed to rest untouched in museums and archives without any effort to translate and publish it. The ignorant charges of "mere magic" and "superstitious mumbo-jumbo" consigned many invaluable relics of this great tradition to complete obscurity.

The late-twentieth-century revival of interest in myth and ritual has created an atmosphere far more favorable to Gnostic studies than any previously prevailing. Today we are coming to understand that while philosophy is but a tale told, myth and ritual are reality lived and enacted. Philosophy explains the phenomena of life to the rational mind, but myth and ritual represent the reemergence of the primordial reality that created the phenomena that philosophy wishes to explain. Thus, while philosophy attempts to answer the question "why?" myth and ritual reply to the question "whence?" Depth psychology teaches us that disciplines like philosophy and ethics can at best only address themselves to the conscious portion of the human psyche, but myth and ritual provide a direct, creative link to the unconscious, joining the world of the conscious ego with the deep powers of the region beyond the veil of consciousness.

There is no doubt that the Gnostics made extensive use of ritual. Although hostile critics have often reproached the Gnostics for their internalism, we now recognize that Gnostics were keenly aware of the close reciprocity between internal and external, between inward transformation and outward ritual act. In the Gnostic view, the great hieratic figure of the Christian Gnosis, Jesus, came to make "the inner as the outer, and the outer as the inner, and the above as the below, so that they all be made into a single one" (Gospel according to Thomas, saying 22).

The Nag Hammadi codices have brought forth abundant proof of a Gnostic sacramental system closely resembling that of the later, Catholic Church. In the Gospel of Philip, a work showing strong Valentinian influences, traces of a Gnostic sacramental theology are found, along with a listing of five sacraments, all of which are said to have been instituted by Jesus. Thus we read in saying 67 of this Gospel:

> Truth did not come into the world naked but it came in the types and images. It [the world] will not receive it in any other fashion.

Other statements follow that link the doctrine of images to the sacraments. The Gospel declares that the true divine mysteries of the transcendental regions cannot affect anything in the lower world without the intermediary instrumentality of their images, which are portrayed in the physical sacraments; that is, they are the manifestation of "an image through the image." (This implies, in terms of depth psychology, that the transcendental or psychoid powers, known to Jung as the archetypes-as-such, can only manifest in the individual psyche as archetypal images, and that these archetypal images can be invoked and made effective through properly constructed rituals linked to the qualities of the archetypal image.) The Gnostic author of the Gospel of Philip recognizes, however, that this contact with the archetype is not brought about by the sacrament alone, but rather a personal inner transformation must occur along with the external form; otherwise the latter becomes empty:

The bride-chamber and the image through the image, it is fitting that they go in to the truth, which is the apokatastasis. It is fitting for those who do not only receive the name of the Father and the Son and the Holy Spirit, but have obtained them for themselves. If anyone does not obtain them for himself, the name also will be taken from him. (saying 67)

SACRAMENTS AND THEIR EFFECT

The objective of a Gnostic sacrament is not merely temporary sanctification, as in the Roman Catholic doctrine of sacramental grace, but rather a total transformation, a change into the essence of the Godhead. The perfected Gnostic is not a follower of Christ but a deified human being; he is another Christ:

But one receives them in the chrism of the fullness of the power of the Cross, which the apostles call "the right" and "the left." For this one is no longer a Christian but a Christ. (Gospel of Philip, saying 67)

As in the Catholic tradition, so in Gnosticism the sacraments are said to have been instituted by Jesus:

The Lord did everything in a mystery, a Baptism and a Chrism and a Eucharist and a Redemption and a Bride-Chamber. (Gospel of Philip, saying 68)

Saying 68 refers to five sacraments, or mysteries. The German scholar Schenke, however, in his restoration of saying 60 of the same gospel, has ascertained that the Gospel of Philip also speaks of seven sacraments, thus establishing an exact parallel to orthodox Catholic Christianity. Moreover, the similarities of Gnostic sacramentalism to its Catholic counterpart are by no means confined to the number of sacraments. Other common details are also suggested by the Gospel of

Philip—for instance, the *character indelibilis,* the indelible effect of certain sacraments on the soul, in connection with the water of baptism:

> God is a dyer. As the good dyes, which are called genuine, die with the things which are dyed in them, so with those that God has dyed. Since his dyes are immortal, they are immortal through his colors. But God dips what he dips in water. (saying 43)

It goes without saying that there are also differences between the present-day Catholic sacraments and their Gnostic equivalents. The wider context and spirit of Gnosticism leads one to believe, however, that these differences were more in degree of internal realization than in external form. For the Gnostic, especially the Valentinian Gnostic, the hallmark of gnosis was the capacity to experience the sacraments with one's pneumatic (spiritual) nature, while the non-Gnostic Christian could do so only with his psychic (soul-related) nature. Although the sacraments of other Gnostic groups may have differed more radically from the Catholic, the Valentinian Gnostic sources now available to us indicate that Gnostic and Catholic have frequently used the identical sacraments, while experiencing them in different ways. Gnostic sympathizers who because of their prejudices against Catholic forms could not envision a Gnostic origin for the sacraments, and those attached to the Roman Catholic and Eastern Orthodox traditions who maintain that the Gnostics were radical heretics are equally confounded by this evidence from the latest discoveries of Gnostic documents.

What to the conventional Catholic is represented as a miraculous infusion of supernatural grace into mundane life appears to the Gnostic as an intrapsychic mystery rooted in the *pneuma,* the "spark of divinity residing within the individual unconscious." While the Catholic is saved, the Gnostic is initiated, but the sacramental instrumentality is identical, or nearly identical, in both traditions. Thus in the Gospel of Philip we find an early initiation called Baptism; a later initiation called a Chrism (anointing); a transformation rite with the bread and wine called the Eucharist; then a rite of Redemption, possibly related to a final purification and absolution from earthly faults; and, crowning the entire sacramental chain, the supreme mystery rite of the Bridal Chamber.

THE BRIDAL CHAMBER: MYSTERY OF MYSTERIES

Of all the Gnostic sacraments, the most mysterious and least known is the mystery of the Bridal Chamber. Modern interpreters have endeavored to reduce it to a form of marriage, which is not only unlikely but patently absurd. This rite, which was called by various names, such as the Mystery of the Syzygies, the Pleromic Union, and most frequently the Bridal Chamber, may, once again, be understood intrapsychically rather than theologically. This mode of interpretation makes sense of the following passage in the Gospel of Philip, which presents the origination mythos in terms of the transcendental institution of the Bridal Chamber:

> If I may utter a mystery, the Father of the all united with a virgin who came down, and a fire shone for him on that day. He revealed the great bridal chamber. Because of this his body which came into being on that day came out of the bridal chamber, in the manner of him who came into being from the bridegroom and the bride. So Jesus established the all in it through these. And it is fitting for each one of the disciples to enter into his rest. (saying 82)

To suggest an explanation from the point of view of depth psychology: Jesus, the paradigm of the individuated ego, the archetype of wholeness, has revealed in his being the union of the two in one. As an archetype and prototype, he exemplifies the ideal androgyne in whom the union of the syzygies has been accomplished. His followers must follow his example and also become whole by absorbing into themselves their opposite sexual image. Men must become united with their female selves, and until they do so, they can experience the opposite sexual image only vicariously in a woman; women must be married to their "heavenly bridegrooms," their masculine internal opposite, in a similar fashion. Thus, the sacrament of the Bridal Chamber is in fact an initiation signifying individuation; the grand symbol of the restoration of the Pleroma, or wholeness; the *hieros gamos,* or "sacred marriage," of the opposites within; and thus the attainment to the true and ultimate gnosis. The archetypal symbolism of the savior as the bridegroom; Sophia, the wandering soul, as the bride; and the state of wholeness, the Pleroma, as the bridal chamber, in their personal analogues are thus the process of individuation.

Many sayings in the Gospel of Philip support a psychological understanding of the sacrament of the Bridal Chamber. The author of this gospel presents us with a long series of mystical and mythological allusions to the Bridal Chamber, all indicating that the consequence of the primal separation of the opposites (as portrayed in the extraction of Adam's rib in Genesis) was the beginning of death, and that immortality can be attained by a reunion that could be likened to Adam reabsorbing Eve. One is powerfully reminded of the symbolism of alchemy, in both its Western and its Chinese forms, where the union of the opposites produces, in one case, the elixir of life and the stone of the philosophers, and in the other, the divine embryo of immortality.

In regard to Gnostic sacraments, as well as other forms of Gnostic teaching and practice, depth psychology, especially as taught by Carl Jung, undeniably offers a singularly helpful point of entry into the Gnostic mystery. To be sure, Jung himself seems to have had a real feeling for the transcendental, as many of his insights bear out. For instance, he distinguished between archetypal images in the psyche and archetypes-as-such, which are beyond the psyche. But the psychological model has its own limitations. One of these is the notion that the model's scope is limited to the human psyche, so it does not address the strata of reality lying beyond the psyche.

It would be fatal, however, to assume that the experience of gnosis and the various practices and teachings relating to it are nothing but psychology, for they are much more. Psychological exegesis of Gnostic matters can take one only so far—which may be not far enough. G. Filoramo in his work, *A History of Gnosticism*, states accurately: "The Gnostic self, the ontological ego, the reality that makes one divine . . . must not be interpreted . . . in terms of the blandishments of currently dominant subjectivism." The ontological self of the Gnostic is not discovered by simple acts of inner reflection, or the introversion of consciousness. Filoramo (40) concludes:

> The character of subjectivity takes nothing away from the metaphysical claim to absolute objectivity, which the Gnostic tends to attribute to his fundamental experience. The visionary moments of ecstasy in which it takes place are always meetings with a reality "other than me," the empirical "me," the transient "me." . . . It follows that this divine reality cannot be known through the ordinary faculties of the mind.

Sacraments and Ecstasies

The sacramental rites described or indicated in the Gospel of Philip represent only the latest link in a long chain of evidence proving the ritual character of ancient Gnosticism. One of the earliest discoveries of primary Gnostic scriptures is the so-called Bruce Codex, acquired by James Bruce in 1769 in Thebes. In the more important treatise of this codex, The Books of Jeu, or The Gnosis of the Invisible God,

Jesus is described as bestowing on his disciples three baptisms (water, fire, and air, or the Holy Spirit), after which follows the mystery of the removal of the wickedness of the rulers of the lower world, which in turn is followed by the mystery of the spiritual unction. After the administration of these sacraments comes the ascent of the souls through the twenty-four emanations of the invisible God and through the aeons of the transcendental world to the great invisible God himself. The names, numbers, and pictorially represented sigils, as well as the passwords and formulas of the various aeonic spheres and their guardians, are given, many in the form of elaborate mandala-like designs. Once again, five sacraments are explicitly mentioned, and these are to be accompanied by an intricate step-by-step process of transformation.

The Askew Codex, which is often known as Pistis Sophia after its famous text, contains a good deal of ritual material, including a tractate (an individual writing, of which several are bound in one codex) exclusively on magic and sacraments, which has been neglected by scholars. To mention but one prominent example, the story of Sophia's return, with its many "repentances" addressed to the guardian powers of the aeons, certainly suggests a ritual drama that could easily be enacted in a liturgical setting. The ascent of Sophia recounted here may very well have been a liturgy itself.

In that veritable treasure-house of Gnostic texts, the Nag Hammadi library, there are six major and several minor treatises containing primarily liturgical and ceremonial material. Unique among these is The Eighth Reveals the Ninth. While the initiator here is a Hermetic hierophant called by the name "Father," and Christian terminology is absent, the substance of the treatise is extremely similar to other initiatory discourses using the mythos of Jesus. The text quite obviously reflects profound psychological states of ecstasy and is thus a record of individual spiritual transformation. The following passage is spoken by the initiator after he has experienced a change of consciousness occasioned by a long magical invocation of great poetic beauty:

> How shall I describe the All? I see another Nous [Spiritual Mind], who moves the psyche [lower soul]. I see the one who speaks to me through a holy sleep. Thou givest me strength. I see myself! I am willing to discourse! I am overcome with a trembling: I have found the origin of the Power above all powers which has no origin: I see a well-spring bubbling up with life! I have said, O my son, that I am the Nous. I have seen what discourse cannot reveal, for the entire Eighth, O my son, with the souls therein and the angels are singing in silence. But I, the Nous, understand.

The keynote of transcendental ecstasy evident in this passage can be found in numerous other Gnostic works. A good example is the celebrated "Hymn of Jesus," which forms a part of the Acts of John. As G. R. S. Mead has noted, the text is less an account of the words of Jesus and of his apostles as they reportedly danced around their lord on the eve of his arrest and trial than it is a ritual, probably an initiation discourse, performed perhaps like the Eucharist, "in memory of him." The experience of ecstasy described in the context of the ecstatic dance is, therefore, not just the report of an event that happened once long ago, but something that can be repeated by an aspiring Gnostic.

What does all this mean to the contemporary seeker after gnosis? The records of sacraments and rites in the ancient Gnostic documents direct our attention beyond the cognitive mind, which is concerned with doctrine, philosophy, and theoretical formulations of truth, to a psychic reality that has affinity with symbol, myth, and rite. The Gnostics, who represent the first effort within the Christian tradition toward transformation instead of belief and commandment, approached this psychic reality with the passports and ciphers appropriate to its nature. The evidence indicates that it was from these mystic psychologists and technicians of ecstasy that the exoteric church gathered its repertoire of sacraments, even though this debt has remained unacknowledged for nearly two thousand years. Thus, while we search the works of the theologians in vain in our quest for gnosis, we may still discover much of it in the traditional Christian sacraments, which express, nonrationally and nontemporally and through appropriate psychological means, an eternally relevant system of coherent affirmations about the ultimate reality of things.

As beauty is in the eye of the beholder, so true esotericism is in the understanding of the knower. Techniques of ecstasy are studied with small profit; only their practice reveals their true transforming power. As in the "Hymn of Jesus" the Gnostic disciples were called to join in the mystic circular dance around their master, so the aspiring Gnostic of today is called to ritual practice rather than to theorizing. For the truth and relevance of those words of Jesus are still with us, and shall never fade:

> Now answer to my dancing!
> See thyself in Me who speak;
> And seeing what I do,
> Keep silence on My Mysteries.
> Understand, by dancing, what I do. . . .
> He who danceth not, knoweth not what cometh to pass!
>
> ("Hymn of Jesus")

From Samaria to Alexandria:
Some Early Gnostic Teachers

I f someone had asked the early Gnostic teachers about the origins of their philosophy, they would very likely have answered that it was revealed by divine messengers who came from the supernal aeons to bring liberating truth to humanity. And among the revealers and those who were instruments of such revealers, they would have listed Adam, Seth, Norea, Enoch, and Jesus. Though such mythic accounts of the beginnings of Gnosticism do not withstand the scrutiny of historians, this does not mean that they don't contain a certain kind of truth. For in every age and in every culture, there have been some men and women who recognized that inasmuch as the world's problems cannot be solved on their own terms, what is needed is wisdom from outside the world. These people then proceeded to cultivate nonordinary, exalted states of consciousness to elevate their perception to realms beyond this world where such wisdom can be found. In this sense, the mythic account that declares that Gnosticism came from outside of this world is true.

Historically and geographically speaking, Gnosticism developed at the same time and in the same places as early Christianity, with which it was, and remained, entwined—Palestine, Syria, Samaria, and Anatolia, and later, Ptolemaic Egypt. Since the deciphering of the Dead Sea Scrolls, it has become apparent that at least some elements of the Gnostic tradition go back to the Essenes. The theory of some scholars that ascribed the origins of Gnosticism to Iranian or even Indian influences has now been largely discarded. The lands of Middle Eastern spirituality—with its visionary apocalypticism and revelations, its messianic fervor, and its mystical and ascetic communities—are now assumed to be the cradle of Gnosticism.

SIMON MAGUS, THE FLYING GNOSTIC

The earliest Gnostic prophet known to history is Simon the Magician, or using his Latin name, Simon Magus. Simon was born in Gitta, Samaria—a circumstance that identifies him as a sort of heretic by birth, for the Samaritans were long known as followers of a heterodox form of Judaism, which rejected the Temple in Jerusalem and practiced worship on a sacred mountain in Samaria. Simon was very likely a disciple of John the Baptist, who appears to have presided over a school of prophets, one of the "graduates" of which might have been Jesus and another, Simon himself. A third such figure may have been one Dositheus, or Dosthai, about whom very little is known except that he was of Arab ancestry.

The available sources telling us about the life and teachings of Simon are few. The oldest of these is a brief and hostile mention in the Acts of the Apostles (Acts 8.9–12). In this passage Simon, who has been converted to Christianity and baptized by the apostle Philip, admires the miracles performed by the apostles and makes an offer to buy these supernatural powers from them. (The term *simony*, denoting the sale of ecclesiastical offices, comes from this story.) The church father Justin places Simon during the reign of Emperor Claudius (41–54 A.D.) and recounts that Simon had a very large following in Samaria, where he was regarded as a divine being.

Irenaeus, always an antagonist of all things Gnostic, gives a long report about Simon that is fairly informative (*Against Heresies* 1.23. 1–5), from which it is clear that Simon was propounding a distinctly Gnostic teaching with many of the features of later, more elaborate Gnostic cosmological systems. Simon taught the existence of an ultimate, preexistent God who emits a first thought, Ennoia, who is of feminine character. Ennoia is destined to become the Mother of All, the one who creates the angels and archangels according to the plan of the ultimate God. She is the primordial partner of God the Father, but through her role as creator she also becomes the *anima mundi* (soul of the world). Some of the angels and archangels she has created, however, turn against her, imprison her, and subject her to indignities. Prompted by envy and ignorance, they refuse to acknowledge their mother and are also unaware of a God superior to them. Having fallen prisoner to the powers she herself has generated, Ennoia is finally enclosed in a human body, her ultimate prison. Journeying from one body to the other in a painful sequence of reincarnations, she becomes embodied as Helen of Troy, the archetypal woman of Greco-Roman lore and cause of the greatest war of all ancient myths. Finally, the Supreme God sends an aspect of himself into embodiment to rescue her.

It is easy to recognize in this story the beginnings of the Sophia myth. While no single demiurge is mentioned, the evil angels are clearly like the Demiurge and his archons. It appears that Simon included Jesus in his soteriology, for Simon's followers held that the preexistent God first sent his son to earth in the form of Jesus; later he appeared in another aspect in Samaria as Simon, while as the Holy Spirit he descended in various other nations. The concept of the Trinity is thus clearly present in this early Gnostic myth.

The patristic church fathers, in their usual way, introduce a salacious note into their accounts of Simon. They say that Simon had discovered a prostitute named Helen who became his companion and that he proclaimed her as the embodiment of Helen of Troy, while he exalted himself to the status of a manifestation of the Great Power, the preexistent God. Since incidents of spiritual myths being "lived out" in the lives of prophetic persons are not unknown, there may be a germ of truth here, even if told in the voice of Simon's detractors. In any event, Simon and his mythical Helen became the model of the ideal Gnostic couple, and his rescue of Helen is the origin of the myth of Faust, as retold by Marlowe and Goethe (*Faustus*, meaning "the fortunate one," was one of Simon's honorific names).

The structure of what has been called the Simonian myth shows unmistakable elements of the Gnostic monomyth: the division of a preexisting male-female unity; the descent and alienation of the feminine principle, whose role it is to create the creators of the material world; the fall of the feminine into a state of imprisonment and degradation; and the coming of a liberator or savior who is either the preexistent God himself or represents an embodied aspect of him. The story of Simon and Helen strikes a responsive cord in the psyche because it seems to symbolize the story of the soul fallen into unconsciousness and ignorance. The beauty of the eternal feminine and the magic power of her male counterpart and liberator combine to provide a mythologem that was destined to inspire poets and dramatists for ages to come.

Simon Magus wrote a number of treatises that were held in high esteem by his followers but are lost to us. Two of these were *The Four Quarters of the World* and *The Sermons of the Refuter*, in which the God of the Old Testament is exposed as an impostor and the serpent of

Paradise is a benevolent character. Simon seems to have also espoused a form of the philosophy of the "fire philosophers" of Greece, notably of Heraclitus, since he presented the element of fire as the universal embodiment of divine spirit.

One of the most interesting features of Simon—that he had the power of flight—appears in legends concerning him in sources such as the apocryphal Acts of Peter and a pseudo-Clementine tractate. In some stories, which trivialize this power, Simon uses flight purely to transport himself from one place to another (such as from Palestine to Rome). In others, Simon's flights take on a more mystical character. One such example is found in an obscure passage quoted by the great esotericist and Gnostic sympathizer, H. P. Blavatsky:

> Simon, laying his face upon the ground, whispered in [the earth's] ear, "O mother Earth, give me I pray thee, some of thy breath; and I will give thee mine; *let me loose,* O mother, that I may carry thy words to the stars, and I will return faithfully to thee after a while." And the Earth, strengthening her status, none to her detriment, sent her genius to breathe of her breath on Simon, while he breathed on her, and the stars rejoiced to be visited by the mighty One. (*Isis Unveiled,* 1: xxiii)

The power of flight as a magico-spiritual ability is certainly not unknown. Ancient Indian sources describe eight *siddhis,* or supernatural powers, which can be acquired through yoga. The sixth of these is "flying in the sky," apparently referring to flight of the soul. In the mythos of nineteenth-century occultism, the conception of the astral body as a vehicle of consciousness, capable of "traveling" apart from the body, played a considerable role. Metaphorically, flight represents the freedom of the soul and spirit from bodily confinement. In the Gnostic view, the freedom to rise to the stars and beyond is the result of a nonordinary state of consciousness brought about by gnosis. Simon's epithet of the "flying Gnostic" thus bears testimony to his role as an early representative of Gnosticism.

LEUCIUS CHARINUS, THE GNOSTIC CHRONICLER

A mysterious and lovely figure among the early Gnostic teachers is Leucius Charinus, declared by tradition to have been a personal disciple of St. John, the evangelist and beloved disciple. He is also considered the author, or rather chronicler, of the five Apostolic Acts—the Acts of Peter, Acts of Andrew, Acts of Philip, Acts of John, and Acts of Thomas, which enjoyed wide popularity in Christendom for many centuries. There were numerous scriptures circulating in early Christian times that were called Acts. This literary genre was something like a sacred historical novel narrating the often highly embellished adventures of the first disciples of Jesus. The five Acts ascribed to Leucius Charinus, however, were specifically Gnostic, designed to spread abroad information regarding the Gnostic character of Jesus and of the teachings of the apostles.

It is quite likely that all five of these scriptures were originally of highly Gnostic content, but were later altered to reflect the orthodox position. Among them, the Acts of John and Acts of Thomas are the most important and are also the ones that managed to retain a good number of chapters of Gnostic content. After their initial widespread popularity among Christians of all orientations, these two Acts remained part of the scriptural canon of several Gnostic groups, notably, the great Manichaean religion and, in all likelihood, also the Cathar churches of the Middle Ages. The beautiful passages of the Acts of John include John's vision of the crucifixion of Jesus (titled by one of its translators, G. R. S. Mead, *A Gnostic Crucifixion*) and the celebrated "Hymn of Jesus," recounting the dance of Jesus with his apostles on the eve of the crucifixion. The Acts of Thomas contains the sublimely beautiful "Hymn of the Pearl" (sometimes also called the "Hymn of the Robe of Glory"), which is attributed to the apostle Thomas.

Leucius Charinus was apparently a young man in his early twenties when he sat at the feet of the aged St. John, who communicated to him many of his great visions and Gnostic experiences, along with lesser-known details of the lives of other apostles. Leucius wrote the five Acts probably around 130 A.D., several decades after the death of St. John. We know little else about Leucius's life, but his place is assured among the early teachers of Gnosticism.

MENANDER, SATURNINUS, AND MONOIMUS

The Gnostic teacher Menander, another native of Samaria, was possibly initiated by Simon. He appears to have lived in apostolic times and so would have been contemporaneous with Simon and the apostles. His center of activity was the ancient city of Antioch, where the Christian community was established by St. Peter the Apostle. His teachings appear to have been genuinely Gnostic, for he, too, taught the difference between the Supreme Deity and the lower God who created the material world.

Like Simon, Menander had the reputation of a magician, from which we may understand that, unlike the orthodox, he advocated salvation not by faith but by gnosis. Moreover, gnosis was to be received as the result of definite practices. Menander taught knowledge of the powers of nature and methods for the spiritual human will to purify and use them. The heresiologist Justin indicates that Menander gathered a large following that survived him and continued to thrive in Asia Minor.

Justin also states that Menander had a famous pupil named Saturninus (or Satornilus) who lived sometime near the end of the first century. Irenaeus informs us that Saturninus also taught the preexistent Unknown Father and that he preached about great intermediate hierarchies, including the seven rulers of the spheres and the lesser deities who created the physical world, which includes the physical aspect of humanity. According to Saturninus, the dark, creative powers have incorporated the sparks of divine light, among which are the spirits of human beings. The savior, who comes in the form of a man, defeats the dark powers and frees the light sparks from their prison.

In Saturninus's teachings we also find an early Gnostic story of the creation of human beings that resembles some of the more complex accounts in various later Gnostic scriptures. The demiurgic creators perceive a shining form in the heavens and try to copy it, saying: "Let us make man according to this image and likeness." Their efforts fall short, however, for though their creation vaguely resembles the heavenly form, it is without strength and cannot rise from the ground. The Supernal Power then sends down its own life spark to ensoul the created being. (In later accounts, this ensouling is done by the divine Sophia.)

Monoimus, who is mentioned by the heresiologists Hippolytus and Theodoret, lived in the latter part of the second century. His teachings seem to have included elements that later might have been called theosophic, for they dealt with the role of numbers and geometrical forms in Gnostic cosmology and cosmogony. He taught that the Heavenly Man *(Anthropos)* and the son of the Heavenly Man were archetypes of perfect humanity, for human beings had been made in their image, but in a faulty manner.

The ever-recurring Gnostic emphasis on the intrapsychic is clear in Monoimus's instructions on how to seek God, which he wrote in a letter to a friend:

> Cease to seek after God in created things, such as the universe and its like; seek Him within thyself, and learn who it is, who includes always all things within himself, saying: "My god, my mind, my reason, my soul, my body." And learn from where comes sorrow and joy, and love and hate, and being awake against one's will, and sleeping against one's

will, and falling in love against one's will. And if thou shouldst closely
inquire about this, thou wilt find Him in thyself, one and many, like
the atom; thus thou wilt find by way of thyself a way out of thyself.
(translation by Bloom, *Omens of Millennium* 240)

The somewhat paradoxical ending of this passage holds the key: one
transcends oneself through gnosis, which one finds within oneself.

THE CONTROVERSIAL CARPOCRATES AND ALEXANDRA

Most movements, whether political, religious, or artistic, are determined to somehow make their mark on this world. The Pharaohs left
great steles inscribed with their names and deeds, the Caesars and Popes
of Rome had their names inscribed on every monument, large and
small. Even orthodox Christianity never ceased to envision a "new
heaven and a new earth." The Gnostics, however, were more concerned
with exiting from the terrible stream of history than they were with
leaving a historical record of themselves. Those who are determined to
overcome the world are not the people of history; theirs is more likely
to be a kind of shadow history or counterhistory, containing a few
faint traces of their tenuous and reluctant presence. Jacques Lacarriere
writes that one can pursue the Gnostics, but one cannot seize hold of
them. This is particularly true concerning the physical circumstances of their earthly lives, and consequently, their behaviors and
their morals.

Palestine, Samaria, Syria, and Antioch were the earliest strongholds of the Gnostics, but it was in Egypt that Gnosticism came to its
greatest flowering. The Egypt of the Gnostics was not the Egypt of the
ancient Pharaohs—of somber pyramids and awesome, animal-headed
gods. Rather, this was an Egypt where the spirit of Greece and Rome
had wedded that of the land of the Nile; the offspring of this marriage

was Hellenistic Egypt, in particular Alexandria, the city of Alexander. In this, the most diverse and exciting metropolis of the time, or perhaps of any time—not unlike the great cities of our own worldly and secular culture—few were concerned with the taboos that the monotheistic desert god of the Semites imposed on sexuality, diet, and other behavior. Very likely the Gnostics of Alexandria shared the predilections of their time and place. (They may even have doubly welcomed this permissive, cosmopolitan spirit, for they had a dislike for the Hebrew God and his laws.)

This information about the Alexandria of the early centuries after Christ is useful background for understanding the influential, sophisticated, and controversial Gnostic teachers, Carpocrates and his wife, Alexandra. Carpocrates was born in Greece, on the island of Kephalonia, and moved to Alexandria early in his life. It is believed that in his

Fig. 7. Gnostic gem, circa third century after Christ, depicting Harpocrates, a deity of Egyptian origin who signifies secrecy. Harpocrates is seated on a lotus throne and points to his lips, indicating silence. His baboon attendant symbolizes the instinctual nature. "Barbarous words," intended as prayers, surround the figures.

teachings he followed those of Plato more closely than did other prominent Gnostic teachers of the period. He and his beautiful wife presided
over a Gnostic circle and gathered a large number of disciples. Numerous heresiologists wrote about them in criticical terms. The principal
source is Irenaeus, from whose account Tertullian, Hippolytus, and
Epiphanius derived their information—or misinformation.

Carpocrates and Alexandra were Platonic Christians with Gnostic
overtones. They, too, taught that the world was built by inferior creating agencies. Jesus was one of the few humans who distinctly
remembered his origins with the ineffable God, when he had earlier
circled around the divine Sun. Jesus' power of far memory enabled
him to receive great powers and graces from the ineffable Godhead, so
he could ascend from the realms of the rulers, passing by each of them
and eventually returning to the Supreme Father. Carpocrates and his
followers took to heart Jesus' words that greater things than he did,
other human beings would do also. That is, all souls that free themselves from the constraints of the lower deities will be able to rise on
high after the fashion of Jesus and attain the same kind of liberating
gnosis that he did.

Reincarnation seems to have been an important feature of the teachings of the school of Carpocrates. (Some feel that reincarnation is
implicit in the teachings of all Gnostic schools; it is, however, explicit
in that of Carpocrates.) When we extract the venomous commentary
that Irenaeus attached to this teaching, we get an interesting picture of
the Gnostic concept of reincarnation. A spirit is born on earth again
and again because it is not yet free from the constraints of the world-
building superphysical powers. To acquire autonomy from these powers,
the human spirit must pass through every kind of activity and condition. Thus becoming acquainted with all that earthly existence has to
offer, consciousness becomes disenchanted with the attractions of
this lower world. To use Buddhist imagery, the "thirst" of the soul for

embodiment gradually dies out. This is the necessary precondition for liberation.

Irenaeus implies that, according to the followers of Carpocrates, the Gnostic could conclude this process in one life, making further reincarnations unnecessary. Irenaeus was probably drawing his information from a manuscript of the school of Carpocrates, and thus he was able to quote from it the saying "Agree with thine adversary quickly," along with the comment "lest the adversary again cast the soul into prison." This interpretation is in accord with numerous passages in Pistis Sophia that seem to advocate a similar strategem to end reincarnation. Irenaeus's exegesis of this teaching, however, is little short of preposterous; he says that since to be liberated one has to go through all manner of experiences, the followers of Carpocrates had to commit every vile and horrible act possible in order to be free from such acts and consequently from the world!

On this idea G. R. S. Mead, the great translator of Gnostic and Hermetic texts, comments:

> Irenaeus, however, immediately afterwards adds that he does not believe that Carpocratians actually do such things, although he is forced to deduce such a logical consequence from their books. It is, however, evident that the whole absurd conclusion is entirely due to the stupidity of the Bishop of Lyons, who, owing to his inability to understand the most elementary facts of the doctrine of reincarnation, has started with entirely erroneous premises, although the matter was as clear as daylight to a beginner in Gnosticism. (*Fragments of a Faith Forgotten* 297)

The school of Carpocrates is said to have favored women in positions of leadership. In addition to Alexandra, we know of a certain Marcellina, who became the representative of the school in Rome around A.D. 150. Pictures and statues were used by the school in its ceremonies, and in a singularly ecumenical fashion, for the Carpocratian icons included representations of Pythagoras, Plato, and Aristotle. It is also reported that this school possessed what indeed might have been the only genuine portrait of Jesus. Clement of Alexandria recounts that the followers of Carpocrates would carry the statue of Kore (the Maiden, a name for Persephone) in procession from an underground crypt into their hall of worship on the night of the feast of the Epiphany. (If true, this indicates a recognition of archetypal similarities between Persephone and Jesus of a highly sophisticated character.) Jung thought well of the Carpocratians for what he regarded as their psychological insight; for it is reported that Carpocrates modified the biblical injunction not to approach the altar of the Lord if one has anything against one's brother to read "Thou shalt not approach the altar if thou hast anything against thyself." According to some reports—considered not very reputable by scholarship—Carpocrates and Alexandra had a son named Epiphanes, who died at an early age and was regarded as a divine being.

How should we regard the accusations of sexual license hurled against Carpocrates and his followers by their orthodox detractors? First of all, accusations of sexual sin have always been, and still are, favorite means for discrediting political, religious, or other adversaries. Secondly, there is no reason to believe that a school of Gnostics led by Greeks and functioning in Egypt would have been particularly attached to Mosaic law regarding sexuality. The Alexandrian Gnostics were very likely urbane and emancipated persons of intellectual and artistic orientation who led lives according to the permissive standards of their culture. Compare the fact that pagan opponents of Christianity spouted tales of horror about the "abominable rites of the Christians," which according to these sources involved infanticide and the ritual eating of children, as well as the worship of a man with the head of a donkey. Are these accusations any different from the ones Irenaus and his fellows voice against the Carpocratian Gnostics, accusing them of sexual orgies, as well as magical incantations, love potions, love feasts *(agape)*, evocation of the spirits of the dead, interpretation of dreams with the aid of spirits, and other kinds of magic?

If magical practices of various kinds indeed formed part of the curriculum of Carpocrates and Alexandra, they would have been no more than adjuncts to their doctrines. When the pneumatic (spiritually fully developed) Gnostic escapes the restrictions of the lesser spirits, these entities become subservient to the Gnostic. All magic is based on the ability of informed consciousness to break through the barriers of the lower worlds and command the guardians of the gates of the cosmos. The greatest magic of the Gnostics, however, has always been liberation from the confinement in the regions of matter and mind.

Bardaisan of Edessa: The Gnostic Statesman

To a somewhat later period belongs Bardaisan, or Bardesanes, a Syrian nobleman, philosopher, and advisor of kings. He was born in the royal city of Edessa on July 11, 155 A.D., and died there in 233, full of years and full of honor. He was a confidant of the Abgar dynasty of Edessa, whose crown prince he befriended early in his life. When the prince ascended the throne, Bardaisan stood at his side as his advisor. Like Mani a generation later, Bardaisan converted his king, and with him much of the kingdom, to his faith, which was a Gnostic form of Christianity. Edessa was most likely the first Christian state, and the only Gnostic state, in history. After some decades, the Roman emperor Caracalla deprived the Abgar king of his throne. Bardaisan eloquently defended the Christian religion before the Roman authorities, so that even the hostile Epiphanius was compelled to refer to him as "almost a confessor."

Bardaisan was a man of great culture and learning. He traveled to

Armenia, where he contributed to the local Christian literature. He was also familiar with the religion of India and wrote a book about it, from which the Neoplatonic philosopher Porphyry subsequently quoted. Bardaisan obtained a well-deserved high reputation as a writer on the Christian Gnosis; a master of Greek style and rhetoric, he wrote many books in Greek, as also in Syriac, all of a poetic and inspiring style. A list of at least some of his books is extant and includes such titles as *The Light and the Darkness, The Spiritual Nature of Truth, The Stable and the Unstable,* and *Concerning Fate.* Unfortunately, only fragments of these works remain. In the nineteenth century there surfaced a complete treatise entitled *Book of the Laws of Countries,* which is a summary of Bardaisan's teachings. Bardaisan is also known as the originator of the Christian genre of the hymn, that is, religious poetry set to music and sung during church services. He authored a collection of 150 hymns written somewhat after the fashion of the biblical psalms. His co-editor and co-composer was his son, appropriately named Harmonius. One hundred and twenty years later, the orthodox Christian Ephraim of Edessa plagiarized much of Bardaisan's corpus of hymns, all the while denouncing him as a heretic.

Bardaisan's teachings were apparently not regarded as particularly heretical within his lifetime. It is useful to recall that standards of orthodoxy hardly existed for the first two hundred years or more of Christian history. The Christian Church was a loose collection of communities possessing a wide diversity of beliefs and practices and having not much more in common than a regard for Jesus and his mission. Had the tide of ecclesiastical politics not shifted to rigid uniformity, Bardaisan might have gone down in history as a saint, or at least as a very talented and devoted Christian leader and teacher.

The summary of Bardaisan's teachings in the *Book of the Laws of Countries* shows distinct features of classical Gnosticism. The human being is comprised of body, soul, and spirit. The body is a product of the material world. The soul is colored by the psychic qualities imposed upon it by the spheres of the planets, through which it descends into embodiment. Astrology thus is important in understanding the fate of a human being on earth. The spirit is the divine element that links the human being with God. As the cosmos is characterized by the opposition of matter and spirit, so at the human level there exists a conflict between fate and human essence.

Bardaisan was opposed to the Christian teaching of the resurrection of the flesh. In his view, the material body returns to matter. The soul, on the other hand, has a kind of conditional immortality, for after it sheds its psychic accretions, gathered from earthly life and from the planets, it unites with the spirit and enters the Bridal Chamber of Light. Before the time of Jesus Christ, the return of the soul to God was impossible. But Christ, through his teachings and mysteries, removed the impediments that have been attached to our souls since the incarnation of Adam, and now freedom from earthly bondage has become a possibility.

Bardaisan is in many ways a seminal figure of what later came to be called the St. Thomas school of Christianity. Tradition holds that St. Thomas the Apostle was the first to bring Christianity to Syria, and he is considered the founder and patron saint of the Syrian Orthodox Church both in the Middle East and in India. Bardaisan was also clearly the first public leader of Christianity in Syria, having even brought about the establishment of Christianity as a state religion there. Thus the St. Thomas school of Christianity remains connected with Bardaisan, even though this connection is largely unacknowledged in ecclesiastical circles. The Gospel according to Thomas from the Nag Hammadi collection is unmistakably both Syrian Christian and Gnostic in origin. The same is true of other books referring to Thomas, such as The Book of Thomas the Contender and most particularly the Acts of Thomas, ascribed to Leucius Charinus.

Some scholars feel that portions of the Acts of Thomas may have been written by Bardaisan. Among these is the celebrated "Hymn of the Pearl." The three main teachings of Bardaisan, which the orthodox Ephreim points out as heretical, appear in the "Hymn of the Pearl." Another portion of the Acts that shows great affinity with the thought of Bardaisan is the beautiful poem called the "Wedding Hymn" (translated by Mead as "The Wedding Song of Wisdom"), which clearly refers to the celestial wedding in the Bridal Chamber of Light, of which Bardaisan wrote.

The question remains: Did Bardaisan or his disciples interpolate these and other poetic pieces into the Acts of Thomas, or did Bardaisan receive many of his Gnostic teachings from the school of Thomas? In view of the picture of Thomas as the Gnostic apostle par excellence that emerges from the Nag Hammadi collection, the latter seems more likely.

VISIONARIES AND PROPHETS: THE GREAT MASTERS OF GNOSIS

Ιt was the sociologist Max Weber who popularized the now frequently used words *charisma* and *charismatic power*. He was referring to outstanding people in various fields, but particularly the religious field, who seem to possess a power that attracts, convinces, and enlightens others. An outstanding example in American religious history is the Mormon prophet Joseph Smith, of whom Harold Bloom wrote that he not only saw visions (a fairly common feat), but also had the power to make others see his visions. By these definitions, the greatest of the Gnostic teachers and leaders were certainly charismatic leaders.

Visions are of many kinds, as are prophetic perceptions and utterances. Most people in any age who seek after such experiences do so for personal reasons, and so it was also at the time of the Gnostics. Much of Greco-Egyptian magic is oriented toward earthly ends—material benefits, such as healing the body, acquiring wealth, influencing the weather; and emotional or psychological benefits, such as gaining power over others for various ends. (One need only consider the many contexts in which "empowerment" is sought in our day to be convinced that today's popular objectives are of the same order.) In the Gnostic context, however, the visionary experience is turned into a primarily internal experience of transformative transcendence. St. Paul the Apostle was a particular favorite of most Gnostics because they regarded his experience on the road to Damascus as a transformative vision of this kind, a decisive turning point in an individual's life. Many of the greatest Gnostic masters followed in Paul's footsteps in this regard, for their visionary spiritual experiences were not miracle working but redemptive in intent.

VALENTINUS, A GNOSTIC FOR ALL SEASONS

Indeed, St. Paul was the acknowledged source of inspiration for the greatest of all Gnostic teachers, Valentinus, who is said to have been a disciple of Theudas (or Theodas), a friend and student of Paul. It is no secret that there are numerous distinctly Gnostic elements in Paul's writings. He speaks of "hidden mysteries" and "secret wisdom" that can be told only to those belonging to an elite. What appealed most to Gnostics, including Valentinus, however, was that Paul became an apostle as the result of his own gnosis rather than by association with Jesus. Paul's account of being "caught up to the third heaven," "whether in the body or out of body I do not know," and there learning "things that cannot be told, which man may not utter" (2 Cor. 12.2–4) fully qualified him as the Gnostic apostle par excellence. He was thus an excellent source for the teachings and apostolic succession of Valentinus.

Concerning his lifelong interest in matters Gnostic, the Dutch scholar Gilles Quispel, a noted Gnostic expert and an associate of C. G. Jung, tells a remarkable story. During the dark years of World War II, when life and the world seemed lacking in hope and joy, Quispel turned to the study of Valentinus. The inspiration, comfort, and faith he derived from the writings of Valentinus were instrumental in turning him into a devoted and thoroughly sympathetic scholar of Gnosticism. Very likely Quispel's experience is not unique, and in fact many people in the contemporary world are finding the message of this greatest of all Gnostic teachers highly relevant and helpful.

G. R. S. Mead called Valentinus "the great unknown" of Gnosticism, and indeed there is little information regarding his life and personality. He was born in Africa, probably within the territory of the ancient city of Carthage, around or before 100 A.D. Educated in Alexandria, in his prime years he transferred his residence to Rome, where he achieved high prominence in the Christian community between the years 135 and 160. Tertullian writes that Valentinus was a candidate for the office of bishop of Rome and lost the election by a rather narrow margin. Tertullian, who himself joined the heresy of Montanism, alleges that Valentinus fell into apostasy around 175. There is evidence, however, that he was never universally condemned as a heretic in his lifetime and that he remained a respected member of the Christian community until his death. He was almost certainly a priest in the mainstream church and may even have been a bishop. Tertullian also stated that Valentinus was personally acquainted with Origen, and one may speculate with some justification that Valentinus's influence on this orthodox church father was considerable.

The overall character of Valentinus's contribution has been accurately summarized by Mead:

> The Gnosis in his hands is trying to . . . embrace everything, even the most dogmatic formulation of the traditions of the Master. The great popular movement and its incomprehensibilities were recognized by Valentinus as an integral part of the mighty outpouring; he laboured to weave all together, external and internal, into one piece, devoted his life to the task, and doubtless only at his death perceived that for that

age he was attempting the impossible. None but the very few could ever appreciate the ideal of the man, much less understand it. (*Fragments of a Faith Forgotten* 2)

Valentinus, the Gnostic who almost became Pope, was perhaps the only man who could have achieved positive recognition for the Gnostic approach to the message of Christ. If he had been elected Pope, his hermeneutic vision, combined with his superb sense of the mythical, might have fostered a general flowering of the gnosis within the very fabric of the Church of Rome, leading to an authoritative paradigm of Gnostic Christianity that could not easily have been exorcised for centuries, if at all. The fact that circumstances and the increasing flood tide of a regressive pseudo-orthodoxy caused his efforts to fail must be reckoned among the greatest tragedies of the history of Christianity. Still, many essential features of his unique contribution have survived, and more have recently been retrieved from the sands of the desert of Egypt. The most important of these are addressed in the remainder of this section.

Psychocosmogony and the Pneumatic Equation

The often debated cosmogony of Valentinus is best understood as based on the single existential recognition: something is wrong. Somewhere, somehow, the fabric of being at the existential level of human functioning has lost its integrity. We live in a system that lacks fundamental integrity and thus is defective. Orthodox Christians as well as Jews recognize this to be true, but they account for the "wrongness" in human existence as the effects of human sin—original or other. In contrast, and like all other Gnostics, Valentinus recognizes that the creation has lacked integrity since the beginning, and thus humans need not feel collective guilt for what has been called a "fall."

Valentinus's own variations on the Gnostic theme includes the signal importance that he gives to Sophia, the feminine emanation from the Pleroma. Though the figure of the Divine Feminine was undoubtedly present in Gnosticism since its inception, as evidenced in the teachings of the earliest known Gnostic, Simon Magus, the myth of Sophia in particular, with all of its rich detail and dramatic elaborations, is largely the work of Valentinus.

The first proposition of what some scholars have called the "pneumatic equation" of Valentinus is that the system of the world and the system of the human being are both flawed. Humans live in an absurd world that can be rendered meaningful only by gnosis. Even many of the gods are illusory entities made real by the human mind for its own limited purposes. In the Gospel of Philip, a scripture of the school of Valentinus, we find the following very modern (or postmodern) statement:

> God created man and man created God. So is it in the world. Men make gods and they worship their creations. It would be fitting for [such] gods to worship men. (saying 85)

The proposition that the human mind lives in a largely self-created world of illusion, from which only the enlightenment of a kind of gnosis can rescue it, finds powerful analogues in the two great religions of the East, Hinduism and Buddhism. The Upanishads say that the world is God's maya, or "illusion," through which he deceives himself. Certainly this could easily have been written by Valentinus or another Gnostic. According to the teachings of Buddha, the world of apparent reality consists of ignorance, impermanence, and the lack of authentic selfhood.

After accepting the proposition of the flawed system, the mind needs to recognize the second, complementary part of Valentinus's "equation." Irenaeus, in his work *Against Heresies*, quotes Valentinus concerning this point:

Perfect redemption is the cognition itself of the ineffable greatness: For since through ignorance came about the defect . . . the whole system springing from ignorance is dissolved in Gnosis. Therefore Gnosis is the redemption of the inner man; and it is not of the body, for the body is corruptible; nor is it psychical, for even the soul is a product of the defect and it is a lodging to the spirit: Pneumatic [spiritual] therefore also must be redemption itself. Through Gnosis, then, is redeemed the inner, spiritual man: So that to us suffices the Gnosis of universal being: And this is the true redemption. (1.21.4)

The ignorance that creates the false system is thus rectified by spiritual gnosis. There is no need whatsoever for guilt, for repentance from so-called sin; neither is there need for blind belief in a vicarious salvation by way of the death of Jesus. We don't need to be saved; we need to be transformed by gnosis. The wrong-headedness and malignancy of the existential condition of humanity can be changed into a glorious image of the fullness of being. Spiritual self-knowledge is thus the inverse equivalent of the ignorance of the unredeemed ego. The elaborate mythic structures of cosmogony and redemption bequeathed to us by Valentinus are but the poetic-scriptural expressions of this grand proposition, which is relevant to the existential condition of the human psyche in all ages and in all cultures.

The Gnostic Savior: Maker of Wholeness

The foregoing does not mean that Valentinus denied or even diminished the importance of Jesus in his teachings. The great devotion and reverence Valentinus showed for Jesus is revealed with sublime poetic beauty in the Gospel of Truth, which in its original form was authored by Valentinus himself. According to Valentinus, Jesus is indeed Savior, but in the sense of the original Greek word, *soter,* which was used by orthodox and Gnostic Christians alike. *Soter* means "healer," or "bestower of health." From this is derived *soteria,* which today is translated "salvation," but originally meant "healthiness, deliverance from imperfection, becoming whole, preserving one's wholeness." What then is the role of the *soter*, the spiritual maker of wholeness, if he has no need to save humankind from either original or personal sin?

Valentinus's premise is that both the world and humanity are sick. The sickness of both has a common root: ignorance. That is, we ignore the authentic values of life and substitute inauthentic ones for them. We believe that we need physical things (such as money, symbols of power and prestige, physical pleasures) in order to be happy or whole. Similarly, we fall in love with the ideas and abstractions of our minds. (Our rigidities are always due to excessive attachment to abstract concepts and precepts.) The sickness of materialism was called "hyleticism" (worship of matter) by the Gnostics, while the sickness of abstract intellectualism and moralizing was known as "psychism" (worship of the mind and the emotional soul). The true role of the facilitators of wholeness in this world, among whom Jesus occupies the place of honor, is to exorcise these sicknesses by bringing knowledge of the *pneuma* or spirit to the soul and mind. The obsessive attachment to material and mental things is thus replaced by spiritual freedom; the inauthentic values give way to the authentic values associated with the spirit. Such is the healing work of Jesus, said Valentinus.

Valentinus, Sacrament, and Seership

The methods Valentinus advocated for facilitating a true spiritual gnosis are not confined to philosophical doctrines and poetic mythologems. The Valentinian system was above all a system of sacrament. As noted in chapter 7, the Gospel of Philip lists five of the seven historical sacraments (or rather their original Gnostic forms)—Baptism, Chrism, Eucharist, Redemption, and the Bridal Chamber—and mentions the two remaining ones as well. The Valentinian Gnosis speaks of the two great and mysterious sacraments called Redemption (*Apolytrosis*) and Bridal Chamber. While many of the formulas for these have been lost, their essential meanings can still be discovered by perusing the accounts given by the church fathers and the references contained in the Gnostic scriptures.

The following formula accompanies the Valentinian "Redemption":

> I am established, I am redeemed and I redeem my soul from this aeon and from all that comes from it, in the name of IAO, who redeemed his soul unto the redemption in Christ, the living one. (Irenaeus, *Against Heresies* 1.21.5)

Even as Buddha is said to have refused the offers of Mara, the deceiver, prior to his enlightenment under the Bodhi Tree, so the Gnostic severs every connection with unconsciousness and compulsion, and lives and dies as a sovereign being of light and power. There is every indication that the double sacraments of the Bridal Chamber and Redemption brought enormous transformations as well as enlightenment to the recipients. These rites survived in modified form among the followers of the prophet Mani and among the Cathars of the Languedoc. The latter had a great sacrament resembling the Apolytrosis, called the Consolamentum, which gave its recipients not only a great serenity toward life but a virtually unequaled courage to face death (discussed further in chapter 10).

The church fathers' testimony also informs us that the followers of Valentinus were usually content to be members of the established Christian communities and to partake of the sacraments there. The only thing they reserved was their interpretation of the meaning of the sacraments. It was their conviction that a Gnostic who was a pneumatic, that is, who was in touch with the higher spiritual realities, could understand the sacraments with his spirit. This approach was abominated by hostile church fathers, who regarded it as heresy!

The foregoing briefly illustrates the richness of the Valentinian heritage of wisdom. Philosophic integrity, psychological insight, poetic and artistic exaltation and beauty, mingled with true religious devotion and emotion characterize the contribution of Valentinus and elevate it over most Gnostic and semi-Gnostic systems and schools. Were one to combine the highest and best products of existentialism, one might only approximate the sublime message of this great technician of human transformation who beckons to us from across nearly two millennia. Valentinus indeed lives. He was and is a source of inspiration and guidance for persons in every age and clime, a timeless messenger of the mysteries of the soul.

Hippolytus of Rome, in his work *Refutation of All Heresies* (6.42.2), recounts one of the major revelatory visionary experiences of Valentinus:

> For Valentinus says he saw a newborn babe, and questioned it to find out who it was. And the babe answered him saying that it was the Logos. Thereupon he adds to this certain pompous tale, intending to derive from this his attempt at [forming] a sect.

Valentinus was thus perhaps the first saint to encounter the "Gesu Bambino" in a vision and to have the visionary child identify itself by its most solemn title. As we can deduce from the sneering comment of his ecclesiastical critic, this experience had a major impact on Valentinus, for it inspired him to found his own school of teachings. Like the majority of Gnostic teachers, Valentinus did what he did and taught what he taught on the transcendental foundation of his own gnosis.

To quote finally a portion of one of Valentinus's homilies:

> From the very beginning have you been immortal and children of life—
> such life as the aeons enjoy: yet would you have death shared among
> you, to spend and lavish it, so that death might die in you and by your

hands; for inasmuch as you dissolve the world and are not dissolved yourselves, you are lords of all creation and destruction. (Mead, *Fragments of a Faith Forgotten* 303)

BASILIDES, KNOWER OF MYSTICAL ULTIMATES

When Jung wrote his beautiful treatise *The Seven Sermons to the Dead*, he, like a true Gnostic, poetically ascribed its authorship to "Basilides of Alexandria." This tribute to one of the greatest Gnostic teachers will forever redound to Jung's credit.

Jung undoubtedly recognized in Basilides a kindred seer and traveler in the mysterious aeons of alternative realities. All Gnostics recognized the existence of an ultimate, impersonal reality that is the origin of all. This boundless, indefinable, and transcendental plenum has been occasionally glimpsed by mystics of great attainment, but few seem to have been as familiar with it as Basilides. Hippolytus in his work *Philosophumena* quotes Basilides' description of this ultimate reality, which he describes as nonbeing:

> There was when naught was; nay even the naught was not aught of things that are. . . . Naught was, neither matter, nor substance, nor simplicity, nor impossibility of composition, nor inconceptibility, nor imperceptibility, neither man, nor angel, nor god; in fine, neither anything at all for which man has ever found a name. . . . The Deity beyond being, without thinking, or feeling, or determining, or choosing, or being compelled, or desiring, willed to create universality. (Mead, *Fragments of a Faith Forgotten* 256)

Among more recent esoteric teachers, H. P. Blavatsky in her "Stanzas of Dzyan" (upon which her work *The Secret Doctrine* is based) echoes a similar perception. Since Basilides' teaching career slightly preceded that of Valentinus, it is possible that the latter had contact with Basilides and his school. Some astronomers when speaking of the original state of the universe in terms of the big bang theory approximate the description of Basilides' vision.

The visionary teacher responsible for this glimpse of the ultimate taught in Alexandria probably around 117–130 A.D. He claimed descent in both initiation and inspiration from Glaucias, a direct disciple of St. Peter the Apostle, and also from Matthias, the disciple who became one of the twelve after the defection and death of Judas Iscariot. These apostolic men imparted to him, said Basilides, a "knowledge of supermundane things," which became the foundation of his own gnosis.

Basilides was a prolific writer, reputed to have written twenty-four books of commentaries on the Gospel teachings of the New Testament. He is also said to have written a gospel himself, based on the transmissions handed on to him from the apostles. His teachings are summarized and quoted by Hippolytus, Clement of Alexandria, and Irenaeus, who quotes some fragmentary writings of one Agrippa Castor, a supposed contemporary and antagonist of Basilides.

Very little else is known of Basilides and his school, save that his pupils were obliged to observe a five-year silence, presumably to allow them to cultivate gnosis without dissipating their intentions in conversation. Basilides' vision of the realm beyond cosmos as well as his understanding of cosmogony bear a certain similarity to Hindu and Buddhist abstract mystical thought, and it has sometimes been assumed that he was acquainted with Asian teachings.

According to Basilides' cosmogony, the ultimate reality held "the seed that contains everything in itself, potentially," and from this seed a Holy Trinity of three emanations mysteriously came forth. Then the Great Ruler (Demiurge), called "the head of the sensible universe," came into existence. He rose to a great height in the firmament and thought there was none above him; so "thinking himself lord and ruler, and a wise master-builder, . . . betook himself to the creation of the creatures of the universe" (Hippolytus, quoted in Mead, *Fragments of a Faith Forgotten* 257). The Demiurge is shown here to be limited because of his obliviousness regarding higher beings. In this cosmogony, the Demiurge does not directly create the material world, but only an etheric model for it. There are still lesser demiurgic beings, who accomplish the material work of creation. As the agency and impulse for creation move down through several descending hierarchies, so the impulse for redemption also descends through these hierarchical orders until it reaches humanity.

Basilides was a thoroughgoing Christian, albeit, like all Gnostics, by his own definition. He regarded Jesus as the earthly manifestation of the highest illumination proceeding from the ultimate reality. People are able to respond to the salvific actions and message of Jesus, because within their inmost nature is a divine spark ("the third Sonship"). Salvation consists in the separation of the immortal spirit from the mortal psyche and from physical creation. The consummation of salvation will be when the whole Sonship (the emanated sparks in humanity) ascends and passes beyond the Great Limit. This is not the return of all of creation to the source—or at least not yet. For after the light sparks that inhabit humanity have ascended, the material universe will continue.

Prominently mentioned in Jung's *Seven Sermons* is the figure of ABRAXAS, and it was assumed for centuries that this mysterious hybrid figure was a part of the teachings of Basilides. The writings of Basilides quoted by Hippolytus, however, make no reference to ABRAXAS, although there are references to this figure in other Gnostic writings. In the light of recent research, ABRAXAS has been identified as the name of a redeemed archon who rose above the seven spheres and reigns above the worlds. Certainly this concept is compatible with the teachings of Basilides that are available to us.

Fig. 8. Gnostic gem, circa third century after Christ, depicting ABRAXAS. Executed with fine workmanship, the eight-spoked wheel below may symbolize his chariot. The magic formula AEIOUO and other mystic formulae are etched into the amulet.

Fig. 9. Gnostic gem, circa third century after Christ, depicting ABRAXAS with whip and shield. The shield contains the mystic initials IAO. The figure is surrounded by letters of so-called "barbarous words," which served purposes similar to Eastern mantras.

MARCION, THE FIRST BIBLICAL CRITIC

The Bible has been the great inspiration and simultaneously also the great affliction of Christendom. The glaring inconsistency between the spirit as well as the content of the Old and New Testaments is obvious to the unbiased reader of the Bible. In its surreptitiously wise way, the medieval church made its own selections from the less conflictual passages of the Old and New Testaments and presented them in lectionaries and breviaries for the devotions of its people. The Protestant Reformation insisted on making the whole Bible available to everyone (with the exception of some of the most poetic and inspiring books, such as much of the wisdom literature, which were cast out as "apocrypha"). Thus was paved the path that eventually ended up in the studies of biblical critics of the nineteenth and twentieth centuries, who gradually declared much of the Bible inauthentic. It is not often remembered that perhaps the first biblical critic, a man named Marcion, lived and taught in 150 A.D.

Marcion of Pontus was a ship owner who traded on the Black Sea. He was also a bishop and a descendant of priests and bishops. For some ten years he taught in Rome and acquired a high reputation as a preacher. Eventually he found himself in such disagreement with the mainstream church that he separated from it and formed churches of his own jurisdiction all over the Roman Empire. Although in his day there was no rigidly defined canon of gospels (there were numerous gospels in addition to the main four), Marcion did not accept Mark, Matthew, Luke, and John as trustworthy, for he saw many corruptions, interpolations, and falsifications in them. And if Marcion was critical of the New Testament, he was downright hostile toward the Old Testament, even suggesting that it should not be included in the canon of the Christian church.

Marcion said that while the God of Jesus and the New Testament is a loving God, the God of the Old Testament is a just God at best. Jesus taught a new doctrine, derived from the Good God, the loving Father of us all. The mainstream church, probably in order to claim continuity, or to please Christians favorable to Judaism, tried to mix up the teachings of Jesus with those of the Old Testament, but the result was unpalatable. The only solution, said Marcion, is to recognize two Gods: the supreme or Good God, who sent Jesus, and the inferior God of the Law, who speaks in much of the Old Testament. In Marcion's cosmology, the Good God dwells in the first heaven, the intermediate God of the Law in the second heaven, and the angels (archons) of the intermediate God dwell in the third heaven. Beneath these is *Hyle*, or "matter." The world is the joint creation of the God of Law and Hyle. To be brief, these two made a thorough mess of the whole project, and unfortunate humanity came to much grief under these conditions.

At last the Good God looked down from his lofty seat and took pity on the human race. He spoke to his son Jesus:

> Go down, take on Thee the form of a servant, and make Thyself like the sons of the Law. Heal their wounds, give sight to the blind, bring their dead to life, perform without reward the greatest miracles of healing; then will the God of the Law be jealous and instigate his servants to crucify thee. Then go down to hell, which will open her mouth to receive Thee, supposing Thee to be one of the dead. Then liberate the captives Thou shalt find there, and bring them up to Me. (Eznik, as quoted by Hippolytus, in Mead, *Fragments of a Faith Forgotten* 246)

Marcion's teachings perhaps lack the subtlety and poetic beauty of a Valentinus and the mystic profundity of a Basilides. Still, the essential features of the Gnostic worldview are abundantly present. Marcion's great contribution is his informed criticism of the Bible. One cannot help but conjecture what might have happened if his opinion had been followed and the crude and cruel preachments and stories of the Old

Testament had not been available for the use of inquisitors and bigots to justify their witch burnings, their racism, their condemnation of homosexuals, and many other enormities, which all could be designated as "quite biblical."

Marcion reportedly possessed a gospel that he considered authoritative and that might have been written by St. Paul the Apostle. Marcion considered Paul the first Christian who had a proper understanding of the mission of Christ. This understanding was obscured by the Old Testament overtones of many teachings of the church and thus the pure Christian message as interpreted by St. Paul never had a chance of succeeding—so said Marcion and his followers.

The teachings of Marcion attracted a considerable following. By the end of the second century, Marcionite churches were established all over the Mediterranean and in Asia Minor. These churches had bishops, priests, deacons, and a definite hierarchical organization, which may have been responsible for their endurance. We have reports as late as the fifth century of functioning Marcionite churches, and most of these were probably extinguished only with the rise of Islam. When at the turn of the nineteenth century to the twentieth century Adolf von Harnack and other scholars published works on Marcion, there developed an entire school of German and Czech literati in Prague who openly considered themselves new Marcionites. The most famous of these was Franz Kafka (1883–1924), while others were Paul Adler, Max Brod, Paul Kornfield, and Franz Werfel. The Prague Marcionites were the early-twentieth-century heralds of the Gnostic renaissance that dawned at the end of that century, following the discovery of the Nag Hammadi scriptures. The remarkable fact that most of the Prague Marcionites were of Jewish origin proves that they did not regard Marcion's view of the Hebrew Bible and its God as evidence of anti-Semitism; rather, they saw the oppressive character of these religious archetypes as afflicting Jew and Christian alike. Marcion's legacy thus continues to exert its influence through the centuries.

Fig. 10. Gnostic gem, circa third century after Christ, depicting ABRAXAS with conventional symbols, including the letters IAO. Mounted on a ring worn at one time by Manly P. Hall. (By permission of the Philosophical Research Society.)

CHAPTER TEN

GNOSTIC RELIGIONS: MANDAEANS, MANICHAEANS, AND CATHARS

Few early Gnostics seem to have established formal institutions to promote and preserve their teachings; consequently they could be easily repressed. (The fable that they merely disappeared without repression is happily losing credibility.) Some students of Gnosticism have understood the relative lack of institutions as intentional: since no organization or priesthood but only an individual's own spirit can confer gnosis, there was no need for Gnostic religious organizations. However, in mainstream Christendom, salvation is also a matter of the personal relation of the individual to God, yet priesthoods and ecclesiastical organizations abound. Similarly, there is no real incompatibility between gnosis and religious organizations, as long as these organizations are effectively devoted to gnosis. Certainly, many of the early Gnostics did not see the two as incompatible. Valentinus and his followers, as noted in chapter 9, preferred to remain in the mainstream church whenever possible and formed their separate congregations only when and where necessary. They felt that orthodox Christians (psychics)

and Gnostic Christians (pneumatics) could worship together as long as the Gnostics were allowed their own interpretations of the teachings and the sacraments of the faith. Most Gnostics did not relish the role of heretic; they hoped that the initially pluralistic attitudes of the Christian church would endure and so their freedom within the church would be preserved.

However, the growing intolerance that swept the church began to intrude on such arrangements. Thus Gnostic teachers after Valentinus—such as Marcus, an early and brilliant pupil of Valentinus; Apelles, a tolerant and peaceable teacher of Gnosis; Heracleon, a brilliant commentator of scripture; and Nicolaus, an ascetic master of inner disciplines—were all forced to function outside of the mainstream church and increasingly incurred the accusation of heresy.

We know of three religions that bear a distinctly Gnostic character. These developed independently of each other. One of these is not Christian at all, another might be considered closely related to Christianity, while the third is distinctly and rigorously Christian. Curiously, it is Mandaeanism, the one non-Christian Gnostic religion, that has survived in an unbroken line of succession since biblical times.

MANDAEANISM:
THE RELIGION OF THE GREAT ALIEN LIGHT

For nearly two millennia, a small, unassuming group of people of Semitic origin possessing a pre-Christian Gnostic faith has survived in the valley of the Tigris and Euphrates rivers in what today is Iraq. Contemporary Iraqis call these people the Subba, though their name for themselves is *Mandaean*. The Aramaic word *manda* translates into Greek as *gnosis,* so *Mandaean* literally means "Gnostic." Twenty-five years ago, it was estimated that there were thirteen thousand members of Mandaean communities in Iraq, which does not take into account the fair number residing in Iran. Since the massive political upheavals of the late twentieth century, numerous Mandaeans have emigrated to other countries, including even far-off Australia. Far from being simple fisher folk in the river swamps, as they were once portrayed, they are today the best silversmiths and metal workers in such cities as Basra and Baghdad. The Mandaeans can be found in many professions, as well as in many countries. Kurt Rudolph, a German scholar of Gnosticism, encountered a Mandaean student at a German university.

The mythology and theology of the Mandaeans has typically Gnostic features. Beyond all worlds and realms of manifestation, there exists a Supreme Being of pure and glorious Light, referred to as "the great first alien Life from the worlds of light, the sublime one that stands above all works [created things]" (Ginza, part 1). In contrast, the created world is ruled by a Lord of Darkness, Ptahil, the offspring of Ruha, a female being descended from but rebelliously opposed to the Kingdom of Life and Light (something like an archonic form of Sophia Achamoth). As in other Gnostic myths, from the Supreme Existence emanated many celestial beings and spheres, which in descending order become ever more corrupted and dark. Ptahil bears all the characteristics of a malign demiurge. He created invisible worlds filled with dark, demonic beings. He also participated in the creation of the material world and of the physical portion of human beings. Lengthy poetic writings describe these events and the relationship of human beings to the demiurgic powers on the one hand and to the Kingdom of Life and Light on the other.

The history of the Mandaeans appears to go back to John the Baptizer (or John the Baptist), who taught and conferred his mysteries in the Holy Land in early New Testament times. Yet though he is regarded as the great prophet of this tradition, the Mandaean scriptures intimate that the tradition existed before him. The Mandaean religion thus has no historical founder. The original Mandaeans were probably Jews, or a people closely associated with the Judaic matrix; hence their original sacred language, Mandaeic, which is a form of Aramaic. The Mandaean scriptures regard Moses as a prophet of the counterfeit god and Jesus as a sort of false prophet who did not measure up to the true prophet, who was John the Baptizer.

Mandaeans were actually long known as Nasoreans, meaning "guardians or possessors of the secret wisdom." At various points in history, perhaps beginning as early as the Crusades, Christians who came in contact with the Mandaeans referred to them as the "Christians of St. John" or "Johannine Christians." The Mandaeans did not protest, for this name guaranteed them acceptance among Christians. Similarly, the Moslems granted them the preferred status of a "people of the Book" for they could say that they had a prophet (John) and a major revealed book (the Ginza). It is quite possible that medieval Gnosticizing movements, particularly the Order of the Knights Templar, had contact with these ancient Gnostics of the Middle East and received some secret teachings and rituals from them.

Significantly, the only surviving Gnostic religion bears the hallmarks of extensive sacramental ritualism: a priesthood with formal rites of initiation and a hierarchical structure. The hierarchy consists of three offices: assistant priest, priest, and high priest—the last having jurisdiction over a particular region. The priests are allowed to marry. The modern Western notion that Gnostic religion is "unmediated" and without sacraments thus appears highly questionable.

The Mandaeans have many scriptures, the chief one being the Ginza, which has only recently been printed for the first time by a Mandaean community in Australia. Many of their books contain a profusion of prayers and rituals. Mandaean scripture and ritual are primarily concerned with the liberation of the spark of divinity through the knowledge present in the wisdom transmitted to the Mandaean priesthood by a series of messengers of Light. These messengers are not named, with the exception of John the Baptizer.

Because their rituals involve frequent immersion in water, Mandaeans have often been called Baptists by outsiders, who assumed that these immersions were baptismal rites. What appear as frequent repetitions of the rite among the Mandaeans has caused wonderment. In fact, the Mandaean immersion rites are more akin to Holy Communion than to baptism. Mandaeans hold that running water contains more of the transcendental spiritual substance, referred to as Light, than any other material thing. Even as most sacramental Christian churches encourage their members to partake of Holy Communion frequently, so the Mandaean rituals involve communing with the supernatural Light found in water. Their houses of worship are always located beside running water.

There are two main rites of importance. One is the immersion, *masbuta,* in flowing water, which is always called Jordan. This rite is administered on Sunday, the weekly Mandaean holiday. It consists of a threefold complete immersion, a threefold signing of the forehead with water, a threefold drinking of water, a crowning with a myrtle wreath, and the laying on of hands. All of these ritual acts are administered by a priest. Then the participant receives an anointing on the forehead with oil, communion with bread and water, and the "sealing" of the body and soul against evil spirits. The *kushta,* or "act of truth," being a handclasp with the right hand exchanged between the recipient and the priest, symbolizes the achievement of union with the world of Light. All feasts, even weddings, include the *masbuta* rite.

The rites for the dead are the second most important sacrament. The rites commence three days after the death of the person and continue for forty-five days at fixed intervals. The name of the ritual is *masiqta,* translated as "ascent," meaning that it facilitates the soul's ascent to the realm of Light. Mandaeans pray for the dead a good deal;

almost all regular ceremonies include prayers and sacramental meals for the dead. Besides the ritual benefit, it seems that knowledge of the opposing forces and dangers of the afterlife is imparted to the soul, so that it may traverse the perilous regions in safety (similarity to the Bardo practices of Tibetan Vajrayana Buddhism may be noted here).

Very little was known about the Mandaean religion until the late nineteenth century and the early part of the twentieth century. In 1867 certain Mandaean manuscripts surfaced in Paris and London, from which the German scholar Mark Lidzbarski translated first a book on rituals, *Mandaische Liturgien*, which was published in Berlin in 1920; in 1925 he published his epochal translation of the Ginza itself. His work was greatly amplified and carried forward by an adventurous and dedicated Englishwoman, Lady E. S. Drower (1879–1972), who having resided in the Middle East, managed to befriend members of the Mandaean community and obtain from them some of their sacred books. In such works as *The Mandaeans of Iraq and Iran* (1937) and *The Canonical Prayerbook of the Mandaeans* (1959), she made available to the world of scholarship a true treasure house of information. In later years, Kurt Rudolph made useful contacts with the Mandaeans. Today the field of Mandaean studies is chiefly championed by a sympathetic and dedicated friend of the Mandaeans and scholar of their religion, Jorunn Jacobsen Buckley, whose work in this field cannot be praised too highly. (See also the late Hans Jonas's *The Gnostic Religion*, a work readily accessible to the general reader, which contains many quotations from Mandaean scriptures.)

Mandaean scriptures are filled with beautiful and gripping poetic sentiment. Here are two passages from the Ginza:

> From the day when I came to love the Life,
> from the day when my heart came to love the Truth,
> I no longer have trust in anything in the world.
> In father and mother I have no trust in the world.

In brothers and sisters I have no trust in the world.
In what is made and created I have no trust in the world.
In the whole world and its work I have no trust in the world.
After my soul alone I go searching about,
which to me is worth generations and worlds.
I went and found my soul—
what are all the worlds to me? . . .
I went and found Truth
as she stands at the outer rim of the worlds. (390)

From the day when we beheld thee,
from the day when we heard thy word,
our hearts were filled with peace.
We believed in thee, Good One,
we beheld thy light and shall not forget thee.
All our days we shall not forget thee,
not one hour let thee from our hearts.
For our hearts shall not grow blind,
these souls shall not be held back. (60)

MANI AND THE MANICHAEAN RELIGION

Unlike the Mandaean religion, the Manichaean faith, which at one time was spread over three continents, had a founder. His name was Mani, or in its Greek form, Manes, and along with Valentinus he must be named as one of the two great luminaries of the Gnostic tradition.

The prophet Mani, as he should rightly be called, was undoubtedly one of the most remarkable individuals who ever lived. Born in 216 A.D. in Persia (present-day Iran) into a family that was related to the former royal house, he went into exile with his parents at an early age. It seems that Mani's parents belonged to a Gnostic-like religious group, possibly a variant of the Mandaean faith, or more likely, an Elchaisaite community, where as a young boy he would have been exposed to the Gnostic worldview. In the manner of a true prophet, he had visionary experiences of his own that disclosed to him his future mission as the founder of a religion. The first of these visions occurred when Mani was only twelve. At this time he was contacted by a godlike angel, called the Twin, who asked him to withdraw from the religious community where he and his family lived. The angel also told him that the time for his public appearance had not come yet. According to his own report, Mani received the major doctrines of his new religion at this time. When he was twenty-four, the angel appeared to him again and instructed him to begin his public ministry.

Fig. 11. Mani the prophet and painter. Mani's features show classical Persian characteristics and represent him as a young man. Later pictures often show him with a bald head.

Mani returned to his native Persia, where he eventually befriended King Shapur and his son, the later King Hormizd. Soon after the proclamation of his mission he journeyed to India, where he made some disciples but also met with resistance from the Hindu population. He also journeyed into Central Asia, where he spent several years in western Turkestan, one of them in solitary seclusion communing with Heaven. Turkestan remained a stronghold of the Manichaean faith for

Fig. 12. Contemporary Gnostic icon of the prophet Mani. He is portrayed in ancient Persian style, influenced by Chinese portrait painting. (Oil painting on wood by Jan Valentinus Saether; by permission of the artist.)

centuries afterward. But his greatest early successes were in his native Persia, where the new faith gathered so many followers that it became a serious challenge to the established Zoroastrian priesthood. The leaders of the Zoroastrian community began a powerful campaign against Mani and his religion. Their intrigues bore fruit when the young King Hormizd, a devoted friend and disciple of Mani, died and his antagonistic brother assumed the throne. Mani was seized, subjected to many indignities, and finally died in prison on February 26, 277. His disciples, who secretly managed to visit him in prison, reported that he was surrounded by angels and that he shone like the sun. His twenty-six days of agony in prison were ever after referred to by members of his faith as the "passion" and were rightly likened to the passion of Jesus.

The Manichaean Jesus

At the time of his unjust trial before King Bahram, Mani insisted that he had no human teacher but had received his whole doctrine from a God-sent angel, his "twin." Still, at various times he also identified himself as an apostle of Jesus Christ, whom of course he had never physically met—as was also true of St. Paul. Mani believed that there had been other messengers of Light before him, such as Seth, the mythic Gnostic patriarch of the Old Testament; Zarathustra, the prophet of Iran; Buddha, the teacher of Asia; and lastly, Jesus Christ. While the Manichaean faith is usually not considered Christian, Mani's devotion to Jesus was monumental, as the following quotations show:

> This name Jesus, there is a grace surrounding it. For it is Jesus who gives repentance to the penitent.

> He stands in our midst . . . he is not far from us, my brothers, even as he said in his preaching: "I am as close to you as the raiment of your body!"

> Jesus, thy burden is light for him who can carry it; thou hast made the cross a Bema (mercy seat) for thyself, and hast given law thereon . . . thou hast made the cross a ship for thyself and hast sailed upon it. (Mani, quoted in Manichaean Psalmbook 15, 39, 91)

> Let us bless our Lord Jesus who has sent to us the Spirit of Truth! He came and separated us from the error of the world, he brought us a mirror in which he looked and saw the universe. (Manichaean Psalmbook 150)

These statements, as well as many more like them, could easily have been uttered by any devout orthodox Christian. Still, there are aspects of Mani's teachings concerning Jesus that have a unique and certainly Gnostic flavor. Jesus, according to Mani, is a spiritual saving presence who has always been in the world, although he made a special incarnational appearance in Palestine. Thus Jesus appeared to Adam in Paradise and imparted to him a primal revelation. Adam saw Jesus as "cast into all things, to the teeth of panthers and elephants, devoured by them that devour, consumed by them that consume, eaten by the dogs, mingled and bound in all that is, imprisoned in the stench of darkness" (Theodore bar Konai 8–9th centuries).

Besides a revealer of salvific teachings and a bringer of mysteries, the Manichaean Jesus is the personification of the divine Light mixed with matter. Long before his passion and crucifixion on the cross of wood in Jerusalem, he was crucified on the cross of matter. This is the doctrine of the *Jesus patibilis*, the "passible Jesus," who "hangs from every tree . . . is born every day, suffers and dies" (Kephalaia, a collection of Mani's sayings). The similarity of this concept with later esoteric teachings concerning the divine life hidden in the material world is evident. Consider the poetic meditation authored by the late Theosophist, Annie Besant:

> O hidden life vibrant in every atom;
> O hidden light shining in every creature;
> O hidden love embracing all in oneness;
> May each who feels himself as one with thee,
> Know he is therefore one with every other.

This teaching concerning *Jesus patibilis*, however, should not be interpreted as naturalism or pantheism. It does not mean that the universe and nature *are* God pure and simple (except in the tenuous sense that their substance is ultimately an emanation from the divine Source). Rather, the Cosmic Christ, the suffering Primal Man, is confined, even imprisoned, in materiality, while his spiritual counterpart, the transmundane Liberator, who comes from above and beyond cosmos and nature, continues to collect himself out of physical dispersal and confinement.

In The Gospel according to Thomas, a scripture not unknown to Manichaeans, is a statement by Jesus very much along the lines of the doctrine of *Jesus patibilis:*

> Jesus said: "I am the light that is above them all, I am the All, the All came forth from me and the All attained to me. Cleave a piece of wood, I am there; lift up the stone and you will find me there." (saying 77)

Here also, the command is not to bow down and worship pieces of wood or stones but rather to cleave and lift these objects. Far from being merely a figure of speech, these words may be a request for a work to be done, liberating the divine Light dispersed within material and natural objects. That is, the natural world, like the natural human, is in need of sanctification and transformation.

Mani's Basic Doctrine

The conceptual system of the Manichaean teachings is fairly simple, although the mythological elaborations and details are numerous and complex. It has been said that Mani's teachings are more dualistic than those of the Alexandrian and Syrian Gnostic traditions.

This might be due to the Persian matrix in which Manichaeanism developed, where Zoroastrian dualism had saturated the culture for a very long time. It is true that in Mani's cosmology duality not only arises in the course of a process of emanation but is inherent in the very foundations of being. In the beginning, said Mani, the kingdoms of Light and Darkness coexisted in uneasy peace. While Light had no quarrel with the existence of Darkness and would have remained content existing side-by-side with it, Darkness would have it otherwise. Darkness was in a state of agitation and wrath and decided to attack and invade the realm of Light.

As the legions of Darkness approached the realm of Light, the primal Light needed to defend itself. It called upon the Mother of Life to bring forth the Primal Man (a cosmic figure, not related to Adam or other human beings except in an indirect way). The Primal Man in turn had five sons, and together the six expelled the Dark forces from the kingdom of Light and pursued them onto the battlefield of the lower aeons. Unfortunately, on the battlefield the chief demons of Darkness overpowered the Primal Man and his five sons and devoured them, incorporating their luminous essence into their dark forms. This is how the first terrible intermingling of Light and Darkness occurred.

One may note here the ever-recurring Gnostic theme. There is an emanation of divine Light from the Supreme Deity, and part of it falls into the lower worlds of darkness, chaos, and evil. The Light is trapped there and becomes mixed with substances that are incompatible with it, even inimical to it. The sparks of Light that have been swallowed up by the Darkness then need to be rescued.

In the course of the rescue efforts the Primal Man is freed, and he gloriously ascends to the Godhead. The souls of the human beings, however, have been left behind, along with Light particles that derive from the captivity of the Primal Man and of his sons. It is only at this point that the material world as we know it comes into being. The earth is created as an alchemical vessel of purification and transformation where the Light can be extracted from dark matter. The sun and the moon are both vessels of Light that serve as vehicles to transport Light upwards out of earthly darkness.

The Messenger, who is the archetype of all embodied messengers of Light, is brought forth by the Supreme Deity. This Messenger descends into creation and by way of various maneuvers calculated to deceive and defeat the archons of the lower realm, manages to liberate more and more Light. Whenever the Messenger separates some Light from the Darkness, the dark element falls back into creation, where much of it becomes the vegetable and animal kingdom. Animals, especially, are largely made up of aborted etheric forms exuded by the archons. (Note that the Manichaean Gnosis would not serve as a rationale for "animal rights" advocates today.) The Manichaean proclivity for vegetarianism is based on the impurity of most animal flesh due to its archonic origins. Manichaeans reportedly preferred to eat certain foods, such as melons, which according to their teachings, contained more of the Light than others. It is easy to mock such customs, but is it not true that many cultures and faiths speculated about the spiritual qualities of certain foods?

Nor are humans exempt from archonic Darkness and contamination. Adam and Eve, by imitating the lustful copulations of the archons, dispersed so much of the Light that its recovery became even more difficult—thus the Manichaeans' low esteem for sexuality.

The rescue of the sparks of Light still goes on. The ships of Light—the sun and the moon—daily ferry sparks of Light to the supernal worlds. A column of Light erected by the Messenger and his manifestation, Jesus, also conveys Light along its ascending journey. Spurred on by messengers of Light, enlightened humans help to purify the sparks of Light and separate them from their dark prisons. A great work of purification and redemption is going on in the world, and the prophet Mani has taught human beings how to advance this work.

Why Was Manichaeanism So Hated?

The faith founded by the prophet Mani functioned openly for eleven hundred years in various places, yet hardly ever was it free from persecution. What caused this relentless hatred? No doubt the motives varied with the time and place. Christians, as well as adherents of other religions, were certainly at one time or the other motivated by jealous fear of a rival whose holiness, purity, and graciousness they could not match.

Economic and political considerations also reared their ugly heads. Still, it would seem there was something more.

All Gnostics have always differed from the majority of humankind, not only in details of belief but also in their fundamental view of existence and its purpose. The assumption that the world is good and that our involvement with it is somehow beneficial is a favorite of most people most of the time. True, Christianity has in a rather Gnostic way recognized this world as a vale of tears, and so have other spiritual traditions, most particularly Buddhism, which has as its cardinal tenet that earthly life equals suffering. Yet most religions eventually soften their stance somewhat and make concessions in regard to the darkness of the world. Gnostics, however, would not make such concessions. And while the Gnostic schools of the early centuries were rather short-lived and were confined to the cultured elite, Manichaeanism was different. It was a world religion for many centuries, with a large following, an elaborate hierarchy, monks, priests, a liturgy, and sacred scriptures. One could not ignore Manichaeans or their uncompromising otherworldliness and austere negativity regarding material existence. Thus Christian and Zoroastrian, Muslim and Confucian, and perhaps at times even Buddhist, looked upon the Manichaean as a threat to society and to life as it was commonly understood.

On the other hand, most of the faiths that taught hatred of the Manichaeans themselves had monks and nuns, who like the "elect" of Mani's church had renounced property, family, and worldly involvement. The rank-and-file "hearers," as they were called, of the Manichaean communities led lives of greater freedom than the average Christian. St. Augustine was once a Manichaean, as was St. Ambrose; they both seemed to look back upon their lives as "hearers" with something like guilty nostalgia. The hostility toward Mani's "religion of the Light" thus had no realistic foundation. Taking a Gnostic point of view, one might surmise that the archons of this world felt their hegemony threatened when confronted with the saintly, white-robed elect, who were effectively engaged in freeing themselves from the shackles of earthly unconsciousness. Spiritual evil in high places was the downfall of Mani's religion.

Many wise and pious rulers, on the other hand, favored Mani's faith or were converted to it. Among these were kings of Persia, Turkoman rulers, Mongolian princes, and at least one emperor of China. In fact it was in China that the Manichaean religion survived for the longest time: the last, fateful condemnation of the faith was issued in 1374 by one of the Ming emperors. Faint echoes of Mani's message survived in such associations as the Society of the Black and White Clouds and the Society of the White Lotus, as well as in the worship of Maitreya Buddha. The ancient Tibetan religion of Bön may even have had Manichaean origins, for its practitioners maintain that it was founded by a sage who was a prince of Persia. And in Europe the fragrance of Mani's noble faith wafted through many lands for centuries.

THE GOOD MEN AND GOOD WOMEN'S HERESY

Noble castles protruding from steep mountain sides, valleys peppered with olive groves and vineyards, villages and towns built of stone and populated by an ancient people predisposed to spiritual pursuits, and all of this lit by the mellow light of the Mediterranean sun—such is the setting of the glorious and tragic fate of the Cathar religion.

There is no conclusive evidence indicating that the Cathar religion that flourished in the Languedoc in the twelfth and thirteenth centuries had originated with the prophet Mani, but the possibility certainly exists. *Medieval Manichee* was the name applied to the Cathars by Sir Steven Runciman (1947). And Manichaeanism was the best-known Gnostic religion. After a certain time, all Gnostic spirituality was classified by its opponents as Manichaean. The fourth-century Spanish bishop Priscillian of Avila, a Christian of Gnostic tendencies, was burnt at the stake as a "Manichee." His diocese included what once was called Aquitania, where the Languedoc is located. Perhaps, his legacy as the first "burnt one" had something to do with the rise of the religion now primarily known as that of the Cathars.

Historians tell us that the Cathars of southwestern and western Europe received their teachings from the East. In the last century of the first thousand years A.D., a Bulgarian priest by the name of Bogomil had preached in his homeland a Gnostic faith that by the eleventh and twelfth centuries had spread to other Balkan countries and to Asia Minor. Though subject to many persecutions, the Bogomils were a persistent religious group; in Bosnia, where their belief system became the state religion, they endured until the Turkish occupation in the fifteenth century. (Bosnian Bogomils converted in large numbers to Islam and constituted the core of Bosnia's Muslim population.) What is known of the Bogomils discloses that they were thoroughgoing Gnostics, although their teachings bore a somewhat harsher and heavier character than the more philosophical Gnosis of their ancient forebears in Alexandria.

Bulgarian missionaries were definitely involved in stimulating the Gnostic religious revival in Europe that began in the twelfth century. Whether, however, the great upsurge of Gnosticism centered in the Languedoc was purely due to evangelization from the Balkans is not certain. The region of the Pyrenees had long been known as a seat of unorthodox and esoteric spiritual trends. It is possible that the seeds of older traditions were brought to germination by the fertilizing influence of the Bogomil visitors. We do know that close to the year 1172 a number of initiated Cathar *perfecti*, or "perfect ones," gathered in the small town of St. Feliz-de-Caraman, some thirty kilometers from

Toulouse. Under the leadership of a Bogomil bishop from Constantinople by the name of Niketas, they undertook a great reorganization of the already existing Cathar movement and devised strategies for the spreading of the faith. The great medieval Gnostic religious movement was now on its way.

The name *Cathar*, which translates as "pure" or "the pure one," derives from the Greek and was used by sympathetic outsiders to describe the members of the religion. The Cathars themselves simply referred to themselves as "Christians," or sometimes as "true Christians." (A corruption of the word *Cathar* is responsible for the official German term for heretic: *Ketzer*.) Since some of the earliest Cathars resided in the city of Albi, the name *Albigensian* was also common. The population of the Languedoc simply and emphatically called the Cathars "the Good Men and the Good Women."

The Gospel of the Pure Ones

As might be expected, the Gnosticism of the Cathars was adapted to the mentality and worldview of medieval Christians. The Demiurge of the Gnostics here simply became Lucifer, or Satan, the evil archangel. The physical world, said the Cathars, is largely the domain of the evil one, who holds the souls of humans captive until they heed the liberating message of Christ, who came to free them and take them back to his heavenly kingdom. Unredeemed souls are reborn time and again in bodies of flesh, until they take advantage of the liberating message and mysteries of the savior. The supreme means of liberation administered by the Cathar church was the sacrament of the Consolamentum, which acted as ordination, last rites, and the Gnostic Redemption and Bridal Chamber rites all in one. By this rite an ordinary believer would become a "perfect one" and would receive assurance of final liberation. The status of perfecti was open to both men and women, and in fact many illustrious women performed great deeds, both spiritual and material, within the Cathar church. As in the church of Mani, so here also, the majority of the community were allowed to lead lives in the world with very few restrictions. It was not uncommon, however, for both men and women of mature years, after their child raising and other family obligations were fulfilled, to request the Consolamentum and enter the ranks of the perfecti.

The Cathar Church was divided into geographical regions, each presided over by a bishop. Bishops were assisted in their duties by two officials, known as the elder son and the younger son. At the demise of the bishop, the elder son would become bishop and the younger son would advance to elder son. Deacons, who carried on much of the work of visitation and evangelization, were associated with each bishop. Among festivals, Pentecost occupied a prominent position, since the Cathars were very devoted to the Holy Spirit. The Cathars built no churches but held their convocations in large houses, often in the castles of the nobility. A table covered with white linen and adorned with many candles was their altar.

Cathars regarded the human soul as angelic in nature. They taught that the purely spiritual souls of humans had been stolen by Lucifer and confined by him in human bodies, which are corrupt by nature. Thus here, as in all Gnostic systems, the human being consists of part spirit and part corrupted substance. Attachment to earthly things, including sexual desire, was considered the result of the contaminated conditions of human life. The perfecti led lives of ascetic renunciation, which included radical modification of their diet. Some sources indicate that the Cathar perfecti were vegetarians, while others say that they discouraged raising animals for food and thus lived on "what moved in forest and stream." Noblemen and ladies raised in great luxury joined the ranks of the perfecti in great numbers and lived lives of simplicity and discipline.

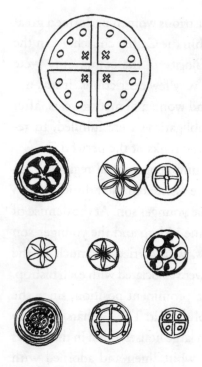

Fig. 13. Cathar symbolic designs, copied from carvings on stones and amulets. The majority show designs containing the numbers four and six, indicating balance and harmony.

The lifestyle of the Good Men and Good Women aroused the ire of Catholic churchmen, whose monasteries and nunneries were often notoriously corrupt. Thus the fate of the Cathars was sealed by the antagonism and jealousy of the church. In 1179 Pope Alexander III anathematized the Cathars, which means that he in fact rendered them burnable. Concerted efforts were made by churchmen, primarily by leading members of the Cistercian order—notably Arnaud Amaric, Abbot of Citeaux, and the papal legate, Peter of Castelnau—to reconvert the Cathars to the Catholic faith. The populace of the Languedoc viewed the proud and wealthy prelates with disdain and compared them unfavorably with the humble perfecti.

Another antagonist was Dominic de Guzman (1172–1221), better known as St. Dominic. In 1206, this fanatical Spaniard was commissioned by the next pope, Innocent III, to take charge of the spiritual combat against the Cathars. In 1207, he faced the formidable Cathar master, Guilhabert de Castres, in the famous debate of Fanjeaux. Dominic lost the debate and thus the chance to reconvert the Cathars. He departed angrily, vowing revenge.

The opportunity for revenge was swift in coming. In 1208, soon after Dominic had departed from the Languedoc, armed Cathar

Fig. 14. Cathar symbolic designs, showing different variations of the circle and the encircled cross. The designs symbolize the eternal and balanced qualities of the Gnostic *pleroma.*

sympathizers killed the papal legate, Peter of Castelnau. Innocent III seized this incident as a reason to preach a crusade against the Cathars, the first and only crusade ever conducted against fellow Christians. Soon the infamous Holy Inquisition was instituted, specifically to hunt and exterminate Cathars. This unsavory institution was put in the charge of members of the Dominican order, who were generally hated even by many Catholics and were routinely referred to as the "dogs of God" *(Domini canis)*. Benefits, both spiritual and material, were promised to anyone who enlisted in the crusade against the heretics. The terrible Albigensian crusades began.

For the Cathars, to kill, even in self-defense, was contrary to the dictates of their faith. The life of the perfecti was devoted solely to acts of religious service and spiritual practice. Clad in their long black robes, the Good Men and Good Women crisscrossed the land preaching what they believed was the Gospel of Pure Christianity. Their residences, which resembled the humbler monasteries, were places of constant prayer and meditation. The high nobility were particularly inclined toward the Cathar faith, but townspeople and peasants were drawn to this form of Gnosticism also. Their compatriots who remained in the Catholic Church held the Cathars in esteem and affection. In fact the Catholic men of the Languedoc often came forward to defend the Cathar perfecti with their swords and lives.

A Gentle Faith Exterminated

From 1209 until almost 1250, wave upon wave of crusading armies poured into the Languedoc. The ruling counts of Toulouse made desperate attempts to stall and avert the slaughter of their subjects. The inhabitants of the country fought and suffered heroically. Often Catholics were slaughtered along with Cathars, as in the infamous instance at Béziers, where the command to put everyone to the sword was given, accompanied by the words: "God will know his own!" This remark, apocryphal though it might be, characterizes the barbaric spirit of the Albigensian crusade.

Minerve, Béziers, Carcassonne, Toulouse, Puivert, Puylaurens, and many more were the castles and cities, the towns and hamlets, where the bloody battles were fought. The siege and defeat of every castle and town was usually followed by a mass burning of heretics. The lovely fragrance of the Mediterranean flora of the country mingled with the acrid smoke of burning human flesh. The savage soldiers from the north, including Bretons, Flemings, and even Balts and Englishmen, delighted in the despoiling of one of the most beautiful and cultured lands of all Europe. Led in the beginning by the grim and cruel Simon de Montfort, whose orthodoxy was exceeded only by his greed, whereby he amassed lands and castles for his personal enrichment, the crusaders left behind an impression so loathsome that it endures in the region to this day. Montfort was killed during the siege of Toulouse by a catapult handled by a heroic local woman, but his place was taken by commanders equally fierce and inhumane.

Undoubtedly the most sacred place, and the most tragic place of defeat and death, of the Cathars was the famous castle of Montségur. Apparently a sacred site of possibly great antiquity, this castle became known as the "occidental Mount Tabor" of the Cathars. Restored by the Cathar leader Guilhabert de Castres in concert with the great adeptess, Countess Esclaremonde de Foix, this remarkable structure sits atop a gigantic rock (the *pog*) in the high mountains of the Ariege. In 1243–1244 it endured a lengthy siege by the crusaders, after which it was captured in what the novelist Lawrence Durrell poetically called "the Thermopylae of the Gnostic soul." On March 16, 1244, hundreds of Cathar perfecti of both sexes, the flower of the remnant of the Cathar church, were led by their captors to a field at the base of the rock of Montségur and were burned en masse. The place is known to

Fig. 15. Mountain and ruins of Montségur in the Languedoc. At the time of its fall, the castle was breached from the steep side of the mountain. On March 16, 1244, hundreds of Cathar perfecti were burnt on a huge communal pyre at the foot of the mountain.

Fig. 16. Ruins of the castle at Montségur. This fortress served as a fortified sacred shrine and refuge of many of the last Cathar perfecti.

this day as "the field of the burnt ones," and a modest monument erected by admirers of the Cathars reminds the visitor of this event. Three days before the burning, twenty Cathar believers had received the Consolamentum, thus condemning themselves to certain death. All of them mounted the flames joyously, singing hymns.

After the extermination of the last Cathars in the Languedoc, their faith survived for some time in Italy. Secret adherents in other European countries did not publicize their allegiance for obvious reasons.

Fig. 17. Gate of the Cathar sacred stronghold of Montségur. The gate is a late construction, yet manages to convey the mystique of this unusual location. Thousands of pilgrim visitors walk today through this portal as they pay homage to the memory of the Cathars.

Fig. 18. Commemorative monument to the Cathar martyrs, erected in Montségur circa 1960. The simple stele imitates an ancient Cathar marker. The upper encircled cross is a traditional Cathar one. The lower cross is the heraldic cross of the county of Toulouse.

Tradition holds that the legendary founder of the Rosicrucians, Christian Rosencreutz, was the scion of the knightly house of Germishausen, a family that had practiced the Cathar faith secretly for generations.

In recent decades, interest in the traditions and history of the Cathars has mounted. Streets and highways in the Languedoc are named after them, and their memory is held in reverent esteem by both the local population and the numerous visitors making pilgrimages to the Cathar sacred sites. A burgeoning literature in French and in other languages tells and retells the story of Cathar glory and martyrdom. Like other forms of the Gnostic tradition, this noble embodiment of the Gnosis is gradually emerging into the daylight of contemporary awareness.

A personal acquaintance of the author, an American expatriate residing in Béziers, once mentioned the name *Cathar* to one of her local neighbors. The aged countryman looked at her with a strange expression and said, "Cathars, Madame? We have always been Cathars, although we don't talk about it. We also shall always remain Cathars." It is thus that the long shadow of the Good Men and Good Women falls even on our present-day world and life.

THE HERITAGE OF GNOSTICISM:
GNOSTIC REVIVALS

The Gnostic tradition may be said to consist of two components. The first is the tradition of teachings and practice. Since at least the first Christian centuries there has been a definite, clearly formulated transmission of Gnostic character. Whether we consider the teachings of the prophet Mani, or his Alexandrian and Syrian spiritual kin of a slightly earlier time, or the once numerous Middle Eastern Gnostic movements from which today's Mandaeans descended, or the Bogomils in their Balkan strongholds, or the Cathars in the Pyrenees—everywhere we find a common message of salvation by gnosis and certain accompanying teachings.

The second component is less definite. It consists of a certain attitude of mind, a psychological ambience. The church father Tertullian is credited with the saying *anima naturaliter christiana* (the soul is by its nature Christian). Similarly, a certain kind of soul is by its very nature Gnostic. Whatever its geographical, cultural, and spiritual environment, such a soul inevitably gravitates toward a Gnostic worldview. When that psychological predisposition meets the stimulus of some element of the Gnostic transmission, a Gnostic revival is bound to arise. And indeed, there have been Gnostic revivals throughout history.

With the triumph of orthodox Christianity after Constantine, the Gnostic tradition went underground. The final blow to early Gnostic Christianity came in the late fourth century, when the wave of fierce persecution burst upon the followers of the Spanish bishop Priscillian of Avila, despite the pleadings of charitable orthodox Christians, including St. Martin of Tours. From this time on, the ceaseless hunt for Gnostics, usually falsely called Manichaeans, made it difficult for the Gnosis to survive. Not until the rise of the Cathars in the twelfth and thirteenth centuries did Gnosticism in western Europe emerge again from hiding.

In spite of its largely Christian character, Gnosticism had a decided influence on Islam, especially on its mystical schools, such as Sufism and the Isma'iliya sect. The prophet Muhammad himself may even have been acquainted with some aspects of Gnosticism, for Gnostic religious groups were plentiful in his time, and people belonging to these frequently converted to Islam. The prophet of Islam is credited with saying that the Christians destroyed the true gospels of Jesus and substituted corrupt ones instead. Could he have been referring to the Gnostic gospels? Possibly so. The great Sufi master Shurawardi, in *Philosophy of Illumination* (1186), freely acknowledged the Platonic and Gnostic sources of his illumination. To this day, the Gnostic element in Sufism is there for all to see.

GNOSIS, REFORMATION, AND POST-REFORMATION

The Protestant Reformation had some tenuous links to Gnosticism. Luther was aware that the essentially Gnostic regard for personal spiritual experience had largely disappeared from the Catholic Church of his time, and he wished to restore it. His intention was ill-fated, however. The unholy alliance of the power-hungry German princes and the prosaic Lutheran clergy soon stifled the stirrings of Gnosticism in the Protestant heartland. As Gnostic or even moderately mystical ideas and practices disappeared from the reformed faith, esoteric sects that were more than a little Gnostic in nature began to rise in Germany outside the state church.

An important German Gnostic figure of this time was the mystic shoemaker of Görlitz, Jacob Boehme (1575–1624). Relentlessly harassed by the local Lutheran clergy, this inspired rural savant wrote a number of mystical books, which became popular among esoterically inclined persons all over Europe. Boehme's philosophy was inspired by his own mystical experiences, but his writings show that he was well-read in the lore of alternative mystical thought. By this time the Renaissance, with its revival of Hermetic and Kabbalistic wisdom, had taken place, giving an impetus to alchemy. Boehme was familiar with all of these esoteric disciplines, and he integrated them into his own system of Gnosis. He taught that the human spirit is a divine fire that has sprung out of God's essence. Imprisoned in darkness where it experiences great anguish and sadness, the destiny of this spirit is to be reunited with the primal light of the Divine. The flame of love is the uniting force through which the human spirit may reach its divine source. Boehme's decidedly Gnostic teachings had a great influence on individuals as diverse as the French mystic Saint-Martin, the Quaker George Fox, and the Theosophist Madame Blavatsky.

One of the most romantic and mysterious developments of the post-Reformation period concerns the saga of the Rosicrucians. In 1614 in Cassel, Germany, a small book was published, the long title of which came to be known in brief as the *Fama Fraternitatis* (Story of the

Brotherhood) or just as the *Fama*. In this book, the anonymous author exhorted the learned men of Europe to band together in an association dedicated to reforming universal knowledge along spiritual lines. The author offered the assistance in this task of a hitherto unknown brotherhood, the Rosicrucians.

To establish a background for this request, the *Fama* spins the romantic tale of a German nobleman, Christian Rosencreutz (Rosy Cross), who is said to have lived from 1378 to 1484. As a young man he had journeyed to Morocco, where he met and received instruction from outstanding adepts in the mystical disciplines. After his return to Europe, he gathered around him a small assembly of like-minded men and founded the Rosicrucian Order. After his death, the Rosicrucians continued in secret, until a hundred years had passed. Then, following the original instructions of their founder, the members entered his tomb, where they found not only the uncorrupted body of the founder but also a number of mysterious objects and documents, which inspired them to give up their secrecy and come forth as an active association once more. Thus the time had come for the order to be publicly known once again.

The *Fama* was followed a year later by another writing, the *Confession of the Rosicrucian Fraternity*. Yet in spite of these and other publications, the alleged secret fraternity apparently decided to remain secret. People searched for the brothers of the order everywhere but never discovered anyone. The skeptical put the entire matter down to a hoax, while others continued their search. In the eighteenth century, prompted by the impetus of the Enlightenment, a Rosicrucian order associated with the then novel and popular Freemasonry movement became active. This revived Rosicrucian association had among its members the elite of German society, including one king of Prussia. The conservative political tone of the order annoyed the more revolutionary-minded who were also attracted to the Rosicrucian romance.

The *Fama,* however, called for a universal reformation of knowledge rather than a revolutionary altering of society.

Whether the original Rosicrucian order ever existed remains uncertain. That the Rosicrucian mythos became an important archetypal motif in esoteric thought is unquestionable. It is here that its connection to Gnosticism can be looked for. The Rosicrucian documents clearly have an alchemical basis; one of these, *The Chymical Marriage of Christian Rosencreutz,* depicts the process of alchemical conjunction. Alchemy, as the researches of Jung revealed, has a close connection with Gnosticism. Moreover, the mysterious Christian Rosencreutz may very well have been a German Cathar who wished to establish a Gnostic tradition with a new format. The twentieth-century pioneering French researcher on the Cathars, Maurice Magre, writes in *The Return of the Magi* (91):

> So of the great Albigensian forest, which was cut down and reduced to ashes, there survived but one man, who was to perpetuate the doctrine by transforming it. . . . From the Albigenses there sprang in the middle of the Fourteenth Century the wise man who is known under the symbolic name of Christian Rosencreutz and who was the last descendant of the German family of Germishausen (or Germelshusen). There is no written text, no historical proof. How could there be?

Magre was deeply immersed in the esoteric traditions of France and may have been privy to oral traditions not known to others. In any event, there continued an ongoing association between various Rosicrucian revival movements and the Gnostic tradition, and this in itself is significant.

Fig. 19. Cathar medallions from Montségur. The six-petaled floral-stellar design is very similar to motifs found on ancient Gnostic amulets. The encircled, equal-armed cross symbolizes ultimate fullness and harmony.

THE GNOSTIC SEEDS OF ENLIGHTENMENT AND REVOLUTION

The enlightenment sought by the Gnostics was not the same as the ideals and objectives of the eighteenth-century Enlightenment. Gnostic enlightenment, or gnosis, is understood as salvific spiritual insight. The enlightenment of Voltaire and his fellow *philosophes* was the exorcising of the obscurantism and dogmatism of the medieval Church. Yet the two were connected in both their origins and their basic direction. To understand the Gnostic component of the Enlightenment it is necessary to look to an earlier era, the late Middle Ages.

One cannot travel anywhere in the fair land of France without encountering traces of the Templars. One of the three greatest knightly orders of the Crusades (the other two being the Knights of Malta and the Teutonic Knights), the Templars were always predominantly French, and their buildings and churches remind the traveler of the great power and wealth this order of soldier-monks once possessed.

Founded in the twelfth century in the Holy Land, the order was initially devoted to sheltering and defending pilgrims to the sacred sites. Some of its prominent founding knights seem to have been inclined toward esoteric spirituality, and such tendencies continued within the order until its tragic end. Hugues de Payens, the first leader of the Templars, had shown an interest in the Cathar heresy, the teachings of

Fig. 20. Cathar stele, possibly a grave marker. The design shows a tree, culminating in a twelve-petaled floral design. It may be symbolic of the zodiac.

which were explained to him by his fellow Templar, Geoffroy de Saint-Adhemar (sometimes mistakenly written "Saint-Omer"), who was a native of the Languedoc. It is also likely that the early Knights Templar were acquainted with the doctrines of the Order of the Assassins, an Isma'ili mystical-military association headed by a visionary guru, called the Old Man of the Mountain. Most important, the early Templars seem to have encountered in the Holy Land, or in places nearby, a Gnostic group attached to the mysteries of St. John the Baptist—in all likelihood a Mandaean community. From these sources the Templars gathered teachings that they covertly imported into Europe, more particularly, into their French homeland.

The founders of the Templar order had a mighty patron among orthodox Catholics in St. Bernard of Clairvaux, whose mystical teachings concerning the mysterious Lady in the Song of Songs are themselves not without esoteric overtones. With Bernard's help, the Templars became well-established and were subject to trial only by the Pope. Their wealth grew, as did the envy directed toward them by the kings of France.

The relationship of the knights with the French monarchy was not improved by the fact that the Templars abstained from participating in the crusade against the Cathars. Thus half a century later, on October 13, 1307, by the collusion of the French king and the Pope (a Frenchman beholden to the king), the order was dissolved and its leading officers arrested. Sometime later, the Grand Master, Jacques de Molay, along with numerous leading knights, was burnt at the stake for heresy. A fearful persecution of the knights followed, and only in a few foreign countries did a handful of the knights survive. The great Templar order was no more.

The Templars' disbandment and martyrdom occurred within memory of the destruction of the Languedoc and the holocaust of the Cathar Gnostics. But while the fearful events of the Languedoc occurred in a small corner of the land, virtually foreign at that time to most of the French, the murder of the Templars concerned the whole people of France. The revulsion felt against the king and the Pope was great and lasting. As the church had revealed itself in the war against the Cathars as a cruel and barbarous institution, so the king now appeared as an ingrate tyrant who had had his most illustrious subjects murdered. The seeds of a radical dissatisfaction with throne and altar were thus sown in France.

Four hundred years is a long time, yet it took that long for these seeds to come to fruition. First, the French intelligentsia became determined to roll back the power of the church and the Bourbon monarchy. In order to accomplish this, they used the pen rather than the sword. Their writings let loose a floodtide of ideas, all of them critical of the church and some critical of the monarchy as well. The second step occurred with the outbreak of the French Revolution. When Louis XVI was led by his executioners to the scaffold, he is said to have stated: "This is the revenge of Jacques de Molay."

This interpretation of French history, while certainly not normative, is firmly held in esoteric circles in France and other parts of Europe. Among historians, Zoe Oldenbourg, pioneering writer about the Cathars, makes several statements in *Massacre at Montségur* that are virtually identical with this theory.

GNOSTICS OF THE ENLIGHTENMENT

By the eighteenth century, more than a millennium had elapsed since anyone had dared to say anything favorable about the Manichaeans. The first person to do so was none other than Voltaire. In his *Candide*, he depicts an old traveling scholar named Martin who is a Manichaean and who successfully argues against the facile optimism of the adage that "all is best in this best of possible worlds." And in his short story "Plato's Dream," Voltaire shows a good knowledge of Gnostic teachings, which he mentions in a favorable tone.

One of the towering figures of the age of Enlightenment was Johann Wolfgang von Goethe, known to this day in German-speaking lands as the poet of princes and prince of poets. Unlike Voltaire, he openly practiced esoteric disciplines, particularly alchemy. He wrote a famous verse about the Cathars, which translated says: "There were those who knew the Father. What became of them? Oh, they took them and burned them!" Goethe's chief work, of course, is his *Faust*. As noted in chapter 8, the figure of Faust was inspired by the image of the early Gnostic teacher Simon Magus, one of whose honorific names was *Faustus*. While in Christopher Marlowe's sixteenth-century play, the single earlier attempt to portray the ancient Gnostic magician, conventional Christian theological views prevail when Faust is consigned to eternal damnation, Goethe's Faust does not suffer such a fate but is redeemed by way of the Eternal Feminine—a likely allusion to the Gnostic Sophia.

Goethe's equal in all respects in English literature is of course William Blake. Blake's friend, Henry Crabb Robinson, recorded that Blake often "repeated the doctrine of the Gnostics." Others have also commented on the Gnostic character of Blake's work, and Blake's own comments recorded by others besides Robinson point in the same direction. Blake had no use for Newton's well-ordered and clock-like cosmos. (One wonders how Blake would react to the challenge that chaos theory and other postmodern developments present to classical science.) On one occasion Blake said: "Nature is the work of the Devil." To him "Nature" meant the whole of creation.

Even Blake's most childlike, popular poem, "The Tyger," asks in a most Gnostic fashion in the second couplet: "What immortal hand or eye / Dare frame thy fearful symmetry?" The tacit answer is that it is the Demiurge, who appears again and again in Blake's works as Urthona (Earth Owner), the Ancient of Days, and under other names. The theme of the world as the inferior creation of inferior beings who themselves become imprisoned by their own creation is most clearly stated by Blake: "The Giants who formed this world into its sensual existence and now seem to live in it in chains, are in truth the cause of its life and the source of all creativity" *(The Marriage of Heaven and Hell)*.

Blake would have been in close agreement with the Carpocratians and other so-called antinomian Gnostics. In "Proverbs of Hell" in his work *The Marriage of Heaven and Hell,* he shocks pious moral sensibilities just as some Gnostics might have shocked them: "The road of excess leads to the palace of wisdom. Prisons are built by stones of Law, Brothels with bricks of religion." And Blake's definition of "his great task" in *Jerusalem* may be the most perfect poetic definition of Gnosis ever devised: "To open the Eternal Worlds, to open the immortal Eyes Of Man inwards into the Worlds of Thought Into Eternity Ever expanding in the Bosom of God, the Human Imagination."

Goethe and Blake were beneficiaries of the conscious effort of some of the great luminaries of the Enlightenment to rehabilitate the Gnostics and to take away the ugly image foisted upon them through the ages by endless repetitions of the church fathers' slanders. They were familiar not only with Voltaire, but more importantly with Pierre Bayle's earlier work *The Historical and Critical Dictionary*, the most comprehensive encyclopedic work of the eighteenth century. In Bayle the Gnostics of all schools found an eloquent and learned apologist.

A great literary figure deeply influenced by the Enlightenment was Herman Melville. The Gnosticism present in his *Moby Dick* has been commented upon by several writers (Stuart Holroyd and Edward Edinger, for example) and thus needs no repetition here. Captain Ahab may be considered mad in the eyes of his rational contemporaries, but many of his utterances would do an ancient Gnostic treatise honor. For example, in the final portion of Melville's work, Ahab assaults the Creator God:

> Thou knowest not how came ye, hence callest thyself unbegotten: Certainly knowest not thy beginning, hence callest thyself unbegun. I know that of me, which thou knowest not of thyself, oh, thou omnipotent. There is some unsuffusing thing beyond thee to whom all thy eternity is but time, all thy creativeness mechanical.

Certainly the Enlightenment brought a sea change in the views of many of the leading geniuses of the culture concerning the Gnostics and their beliefs. The way was now open to the Gnostic thought of the Romantics and, in their wake, to the occult revival of the nineteenth century.

From Romanticism to Occult Gnosis

One of the direct heirs of the Enlightenment was Romanticism, a diverse movement characterized not so much by a central worldview as by fervent feelings often directed to visions beyond this world. Some Romantics, like Shelley and Byron, had no interest in anything that smacked of God or religion; others, like Wordsworth, cultivated a nature mysticism that would have been unpalatable to a Gnostic. Yet the works of other representatives of Romanticism possess a distinctly Gnostic keynote. Romantics habitually disdained the mundane world and aspired to a cult of the sublime. They exalted the human imagination in a way that would have appealed to Gnostics, Neoplatonists, and Sufis. Their "divine discontent" with a prosaic life and their deliberate seeking of nonordinary states of consciousness might also have endeared them to some Gnostics. In short, there was some Gnosis among the Romantics, although it was somewhat unformed.

The nineteenth century was a period of great change and stress, not only in the political, industrial, and scientific life of Western culture, but in its spiritual life as well. Delighted admiration for the Newtonian cosmos gave way to concern with more complex and at times more profound concepts. Darwin and his theory of biological evolution brought traditional Christian doctrines concerning the creation into question. There was much uncertainty and also much enthusiastic examination of previously unexplored ideas and realizations. In the midst of all this, the Gnostics were not forgotten. In Germany, Nikolaus Lenau's epic work *Die Albigenser* (The Albigensians) recalled the romance of the martyred Cathars, while the biblical scholars of Germany and France began to address themselves to a number of Gnostic manuscripts that had almost unaccountably appeared in European and English libraries and archives.

On what might be called the empirical side of spirituality, there appeared the popular neoshamanistic phenomenon of Spiritualism. Seances were held in the White House, at the court of Napoleon III, and in many citadels of high society, while the general public frequented mediums in humbler quarters. Millions of people became convinced that they did not need the pious assertions of religion concerning life after the grave. They felt that they could know directly—a conviction that resonated with the keynote of Gnosticism.

An important figure of the mid-nineteenth century was the French

Kabbalist and investigator of ceremonial magic Eliphas Levi, whose books became the favorite reading of persons who increasingly called themselves occultists. Levi was not a Gnostic, or at least he did not endorse Gnosticism openly. At the same time, he brought practically the entire spectrum of subjects related to Gnosticism into daylight. The Jewish Gnosticism of the Kabbalah now became a subject of intense interest among non-Jewish occultists. It was in the wake of Levi's pioneering achievements that the greatest figure of the occult revival, Helena Petrovna Blavatsky, or H. P. B., as her friends and followers affectionately called her, appeared on the scene. She became the seminal figure of the alternative spiritual movement of not only the nineteenth century but much of the twentieth century as well.

BLAVATSKY AS GNOSTIC

Born in Russia in 1831, H. P. Blavatsky contributed immeasurably to the revival of Gnosticism that we are experiencing today. This remarkable woman's interests were far ranging. She called her system of teachings "Theosophy," resurrecting an ancient term used by the Neoplatonist Ammonius Saccus. Where there are Neoplatonists, Gnostics cannot be far behind. Blavatsky had a profound interest in Gnosticism, and she commented on the tradition voluminously (a compilation of her writings concerning Gnosticism runs to more than 270 pages). The contemporary student of Gnosticism, who has access to the Nag Hammadi Gnostic scriptures, would be greatly impressed if not outright awestruck by Blavatsky's uncanny insight into Gnosticism.

Blavatsky was not concerned with resurrecting ancient Gnosticism. Her system, Theosophy, aspires to a universality within which Buddhist and Hindu esotericism unite with their analogues in Western alternative spirituality. Much of her terminology is derived from Sanskrit, as are her more popular, practical concepts of karma and reincarnation. By the same token, Gnosticism does occupy an honored position among the traditions that she tried to synthesize in her books, particularly in *The Secret Doctrine*. No one familiar with and sympathetic to Blavatsky's corpus of teachings could possibly ignore Gnosticism or think badly of it.

Blavatsky's Theosophical system necessarily bears some of the imprint of the late nineteenth century and its spirit, even as Gnosticism bears the imprint of its particular time. The late nineteenth century was a period of a certain sanguine spirit. Even though the so-called world-denying Gnostic pessimism is always mitigated by a kind of ultimate optimism that points to the soul's glorious return to a better reality, it was still not very compatible with the optimistic, enterprising, progressive tone of the nineteenth century. Thus Blavatsky did not call much attention to this feature of Gnosticism, though she

Fig. 21. Helena Petrovna Blavatsky (1831–1891), Russian-born world traveler and reviver of the alternative spiritual tradition in the West. She was much in favor of Gnosticism, to which subject she devoted nearly three hundred pages in her writings. Blavatsky was one of the principal founders of the Theosophical Society in 1875.

certainly stated her agreement with many Gnostic teachings.

Blavatsky was certainly a true Gnostic when it came to the Gnostic concept of God. In her writings, she vehemently attacks the conventional concept of the monotheistic God and advocates the belief in a totally transcendental and impersonal Godhead—akin to the Gnostic *alethes theos,* or True God—instead. The Gnostic notion that the Old Testament God is the Demiurge is affirmed by Blavatsky. In some of her statements she "out-gnostics" the Gnostics, for instance, when she boldly states that Yehovah is Satan! Elsewhere she states that the universe was fabricated by imperfect spiritual beings. In short, Blavatsky always speaks highly of the Gnostics, and where she can safely do so, she boldly states her agreement with Gnostic teachings. In fact, in some respects she teaches what might be called a slightly covert or muted variety of Gnosticism. C. G. Jung's statement that Blavatsky's Theosophy as well as Rudolf Steiner's Anthroposophy (a variant of Theosophy) were both pure Gnosticism in Hindu dress contains a large grain of truth.

Blavatsky's insightful, sympathetic attitude toward the Gnostics went a long way toward influencing large numbers of creative and spiritually adventurous people in the direction of Gnosticism. Her devoted pupil, G. R. S. Mead, who was her last personal secretary and delivered the oration at her funeral in Brighton in 1891, under her inspiration became an expert

Fig. 22. G. R. S. (George Robert Stowe) Mead, the great translator of Gnostic scriptures, whose works remained the most complete and accessible sources of Gnostic teachings until the publication of the Nag Hammadi scriptures in 1977. Mead's work was greatly appreciated by many students of Gnosticism, including C. G. Jung, who made a special journey to London to visit Mead and thank him for his work on Gnosticism.

translator of Gnostic and also Hermetic writings. The advantage of Mead's work from a Gnostic point of view was that he wrote about the Gnostics as a friend who knew them and who understood the meaning of their writings. Mead made Gnosticism accessible to the intelligent public outside of academia, which prepared the way for several waves of a Gnostic renaissance.

C. G. JUNG AND HIS GNOSTIC PSYCHOLOGY

H. P. Blavatsky founded the Theosophical Society in 1875. Carl Gustav Jung, whose work was to advance the revival of Gnosticism in a way somewhat different from Blavatsky's, was born in the same year. Jung was one of the great trio of psychoanalysts that included Sigmund Freud, Alfred Adler, and himself. His contributions, however, extend beyond the field of psychology to such disciplines as mythology, cultural anthropology, literature, and the study of religion. His furthering of the understanding and appreciation of Gnosticism, though only recently recognized, is nonetheless major.

From his childhood, Jung was vitally interested in religion. His father, a Protestant minister, introduced his son to Christianity, but Jung was always profoundly dissatisfied with the mainstream Christian tradition. He eventually turned to the writings of the Gnostics, which in the late nineteenth century meant the writings of the church fathers with their obvious bias. It is to Jung's credit that from these fragmentary and often hostile writings he was able to develop a fairly accurate picture of what Gnosticism was. He also developed a close, sympathetic feeling for the Gnostics. As his disciple Barbara Hannah reports, he told her that upon first encountering the Gnostics he felt that he was among old friends.

Jung became a psychologist and an associate of Freud, the pioneer of depth psychology. Even in his early communications with Freud, Jung would often refer to the Gnostics. For instance, in a letter to Freud dated August 12, 1912, he wrote that he felt that the Gnostic conception of Sophia was about to reenter Western thought by way of psychoanalysis. His dedication to Gnostic thought found little resonance in Freud's thinking. In fact, it was a Gnostic inspiration that forced Jung to go his own way and found a psychological school different from Freud's. Jung experienced a series of visions involving a spiritual figure named Philemon, whom he called a Gnostic. The teachings Philemon imparted to Jung concerning the meanings of symbols were incorporated by him into a book, and it was this book that caused Freud's final disaffection with Jung.

Fig. 23. Carl Gustav Jung (1875–1961), one of the principal founders of depth psychology, saw the Gnostics as the spiritual ancestors of his own teachings. This lifelong, highly sympathetic interest in Gnosticism is documented in all of his writings. Concerning his first encounter with Gnostic literature, he remarked: "I felt as if I had at last found a circle of friends who understood me."

Fairly early in his career, soon after parting with Freud, Jung authored a kind of Gnostic "gospel." Like the Valentinian Gnostics—who, however, were excoriated by Irenaeus for writing their own gospels—Jung was inspired to write a treatise in the style of ancient Gnosticism. Jung titled it *Septem Sermones ad Mortuos* and described it as the "*Seven Sermons to the Dead* written by Basilides in Alexandria, the city where East and West meet." Jung *(Memories, Dreams, Reflections)* himself acknowledged that the majority of his psychological theories and insights were present in seminal form in the "initial fantasies" contained in this text. The presence of Gnostic inspiration behind Jung's scientific work is thus quite apparent (Hoeller, *The Gnostic Jung and the Seven Sermons to the Dead*).

Jung certainly resuscitated much of ancient Gnostic wisdom and expertly applied Gnostic concepts, myths, and images to analytical psychology. The Italian scholar Giovanni Filoramo in his *History of Gnosticism* (14) aptly summarizes Jung's relation to Gnosticism:

> Jung's reflections had long been immersed in the thought of ancient Gnostics to such an extent that he considered them the virtual discoverers of "depth psychology." . . . Inasmuch as it involves research into the ontological self, a cognitive technique that anticipates the modern process of individuation, ancient Gnosis, albeit in its form of universal religion, in a certain sense prefigured, and at the same time helped to clarify the nature of Jungian spiritual therapy.

Jung has been criticized several times for his interest in Gnosticism. In *Eclipse of God*, Martin Buber accused Jung of being a Gnostic, thereby implying that he was a reprehensible heretic. In more recent times, Richard Noll, in his extremely harsh criticisms of Jung, uses Jung's esoteric and particularly Gnostic interests to prove that Jung was neither a good scientist nor a good man. The religious scholar Robert Segal, in turn, has accused Jung of "appropriating" Gnosticism in an inappropriate manner by turning the aim of the Gnostic effort on its head. The Gnostics, so Segal alleges, were concerned solely with escaping from this world, and thus Jung's psychological theories about the reconciliation of the opposites, the integration of the shadow, and the like have no relationship to Gnostic thought.

Such criticisms are for the most part disproved by Jung's own statements and by the content of the Gnostic scriptures. Jung did not appropriate Gnosticism in order to turn it into psychology. It is clear from Jung's writings that he felt that in addition to whatever other meanings are couched in Gnosticism, he as a psychologist could see distinctly psychological meanings there. Furthermore, the Nag Hammadi writings contain many references to self-knowledge and to the need for wholeness, so that the thesis of the irrelevance of Jungian individuation to Gnostic concerns falls to the ground. On the contrary, with a slight stretch of imagination, one can envision Jung as a modern Gnostic master who offers contemporary perspectives applicable to the ancient myths and teachings, and who makes his own remarkable contribution to Gnosticism. In particular, the myth contained in Jung's book *Answer to Job* expands and amplifies the ancient Gnostic teachings concerning the Demiurge in an original and creative way.

Jung has been called the last of the Gnostics. This verdict suggests that the Gnostic tradition is at an end. Yet even though Gnosticism has been pronounced defunct many times, these pronouncements have always turned out to be premature. One of the people who taught us why this is so is in fact Jung himself.

GNOSTICISM WEST AND EAST:
WILL THE REAL GNOSTIC
PLEASE STAND UP?

In his postscript to Marvin Meyer's translation of the Gospel according to Thomas, Harold Bloom ("A Reading" 120) writes: "No one is going to establish a gnostic church in America, by which I mean a professedly gnostic church, to which tax exemption would never be granted anyway." I respectfully beg to differ. Gnostic churches have been in existence since the late nineteenth century in Europe, and in the twentieth century they appeared in America as well.

There is nothing intrinsically improbable about a Gnostic church. As we have seen, sizable Gnostic institutions, with ecclesiastical offices, sacraments, and lineages of succession and authority, flourished under Manichaeanism, Bogomilism, and Catharism and do still exist in the Mandaean faith. Mainstream religionists may have considered these heretical counter-churches, but that is clearly another issue. Though it has numerous unique features, the Gnostic tradition is capable of being embodied in an institution, and given favorable conditions, there is no reason why it cannot prosper in that form.

THE GNOSTIC CHURCH REBORN

The story of modern ecclesiastical Gnosticism takes us back once more to France, where for many centuries various Gnostic traditions persisted in a predominantly Roman Catholic milieu. As early as about 180 A.D. Gnostics were numerous in Gaul—the Roman province now known as France. Irenaeus, who was Bishop of Lyons, complained bitterly of the followers of Valentinus in his diocese. France, it would seem, virtually always had a love/hate relationship with the Catholic Church. Every time the church's hold on the governments of France weakened, Gnostic religious bodies emerged from hiding, only to be suppressed eventually by another church-influenced government. We have seen that the Cathar religion emerged at what was then a border of France and that a secret Gnosis thrived within the Order of the Knights Templar, an ostensibly Catholic organization. From the eighteenth century on, the Masonic and other initiatic fraternities, many of which were devoted to esoteric and even Gnostic teachings, played an important role in the country.

It was into this milieu that the ancient Gnostic tradition was reborn in France in the late nineteenth century. Jules-Benoit Doinel du Val Michel, a scholarly esotericist who had been a devoted researcher of the documents of the Cathar faith, had a mystical experience in 1890, in which he received spiritual empowerment to reconstitute the Gnostic church of old. His experience occurred in the splendid chapel at the residence of the Duchess de Pomar, Countess of Caithness, in Paris. This remarkable noblewoman was a friend of Madame Blavatsky and an early Theosophist and patroness of esoteric movements. (Because of the confusion in the public mind regarding the relationship of Theosophy and related movements to Spiritualism, inaccurate accounts were circulated to the effect that Doinel's experience occurred in a spiritualist seance.)

Jules Doinel gathered a following and established the Église Gnostique, which was organized along sacramental lines. The teachings of the new church were strictly Gnostic, and in homage to Valentinus, Doinel assumed the ecclesiastical title of Patriarch Tau Valentin II. In a most progressive step he ordained women to priestly and episcopal offices; he also established once again the sacrament of the Consolamentum, reminiscent of the Cathars.

The new Gnostic Church soon became associated with the Martinist order, reorganized earlier by the noted French esotericist Papus (Dr. Gerard Encausse), who himself was ordained as a Gnostic bishop by Doinel. Sometime later one of Doinel's successors, Jean Bricaud, secured a recognized lineage of apostolic succession for the Gnostic Church, since Doinel possessed a spiritual consecration only.

The establishment of a Gnostic church with its own priesthood, episcopate, sacraments, and apostolic succession, was a boon to the

Fig. 24. Vestments of clergy of the French Gnostic Church, circa 1890. The images depict a male deacon, a bishop, a priest, and a deaconess of the Gnostic Church revived by Bishop Doinel in France in the late nineteenth century.

many French esotericists and Freemasons, who were excommunicate in the eyes of the Roman Catholic Church. These persons could now partake of the sacraments in a traditional manner at the services of the Gnostic Church, which were frequently held within the precincts of Masonic temples. The Gnostic Church thus became known as "the church of the initiates."

By the early twentieth century there were Gnostic churches in France, Germany, Belgium, England, and other European countries. The Gnostic Church came to the United States in the second half of the same century, as the result of Haitian immigration. Owing to its French cultural connections, there had been Gnostic churches in Haiti for some time. At present there are two Gnostic lineages—the French and the English—operative in the United States. The two are in friendly association with each other.

GNOSTICISM AND EASTERN RELIGIONS

The similarity between Gnosticism and some of the great religions of the East has been recognized for a long time. The word *gnosis* is cognate with the Sanskrit *jñana*, which denotes "knowledge," primarily spiritual knowledge. One of the great classical schools of Yoga is in fact called *jñana yoga*, meaning "the way to union through knowledge." Initiation into direct knowledge of spiritual realities is a standard practice of the higher forms of Yoga and is thus well-known in India. In fact, in this respect Gnosticism resembles nothing more closely than it does the ancient religion of India, called Hinduism in the West. Hinduism is not so much a religion, in the sense understood in the West, as it is a family of religions. There is great diversity in this family, such that some members hardly resemble others. Thus a philosophical Advaitin seems to have little in common with a devotional Vaishnavite or a magical Tantric; still, they share a common tradition. The diversity among Gnostic traditions is certainly similar.

There are several specific features that join Gnosticism and Hinduism. One is the teaching regarding the presence of the Divine in the human spirit. The Atman is identical with Brahman, which means that the universal Divinity is present in miniature within each person. Similarly, in Gnosticism the pneuma is a spark sprung from the divine flame, and by knowing the pneuma the Gnostic automatically knows the spiritual source from whence it has come. The Hindu and the Gnostic would agree that to know one's deepest self is tantamount to knowing God.

Second, both Gnosticism and Hinduism recognize the existence of many divine beings in realms between the ultimate and the material dimensions. Hinduism is the paramount polytheistic religion in the world today, whereas Gnosticism functions within a monotheistic matrix. But Gnosticism can hardly be called a monotheistic religion pure and simple. Moreover, some of the Vedic deities of Hinduism, such as Indra or Prajapati, have similar qualities to the Gnostic Demiurge.

Third, Hindu teachings have much to say about what constitutes duality *(dvaita)* and what is nondual *(advaita)*. While Gnosticism is often described as dualistic, its view of both of these categories is actually comparable to the Hindu. Thus, in the realm of what Hinduism calls *maya* (illusory manifestation), duality prevails and the struggle of light and dark takes place, while on the plane of ultimate reality there is a fullness of being, comparable to what is known to the Gnostics as the Pleroma.

Gnosticism also has similarities with Buddhism, the other great faith of the East. First of all, the supreme objective of Buddhism—identical with the ultimate aim of Gnosticism—is liberation, meaning freedom from embodied existence and thereby from all future suffering. (The bodhisattva ideal and other modifying teachings are only elaborations of this basic teaching.) The following list of points of convergence between Gnosticism and Buddhism—specifically Mahayana Buddhism—is based on statements of the late renowned Buddhist scholar Edward Conze:

- Salvation is achieved through gnosis *(jñana)*. Insight into the dependent origination of manifest existence is what liberates.

- Ignorance is the true root of evil; in Gnosticism it is called *agnosis,* and in Buddhism, *avidya.*

- Both Gnostic and Buddhist knowledge are arrived at not by ordinary means but as the result of interior revelation.

- There are levels of spiritual attainment, ranging from the condition of a foolish materialist (hyletic) to that of an illumined saint (pneumatic).

- In both Gnosticism and Buddhism, the feminine principle of wisdom (Sophia and Prajña, respectively) plays an important role. Conze quotes the *Hevajra Tantra:* "Prajña is called Mother, because she gives birth to the world." There are other deities in Buddhism that may be cognate to Sophia, such as Tara and Kwan Yin.

- Both Gnosticism and Buddhism show a preference for myth over fact. Christ as well as Buddha are presented as archetypal beings rather than merely historical figures.

- A tendency to antinomianism (disregard for rules and commandments) is inherent in both systems. While at the lower rungs of the spiritual ladder, rules of behavior are considered important and even crucial, in exalted spiritual states the importance of such rules becomes relative.

- Both systems are disdainful of easy popularity and aim their teachings to a spiritual elite. Hidden meanings and mysterious teachings are prevalent in both systems.

- Both Gnosticism and Buddhism are metaphysically monistic, which means that they aspire to transcend the multiplicity of manifest things and achieve a condition of ultimate oneness.

These similarities may be specially of interest in view of the current popularity of the Tibetan (Vajrayana) form of Mahayana Buddhism in the West.

THE DIFFICULTY OF DEFINING GNOSTICISM

Gnosticism has always been difficult to define, largely because it is a system of thought based upon and frequently amended by experiences of nonordinary states of consciousness, and thus it is resistant to theological rigidity. The majority of scholars studying Gnosticism have been men of religion, and they understandably judged their subject by the standards of their own systems of belief. But Gnosticism was never a religious construct that could be compared with Western, especially Christian, theology. It has always been a bird of another feather—or perhaps a different life form altogether.

Today we find a number of peculiar definitions of Gnosticism co-existing with the few reasonably correct ones. One lone voice (Michael Allen Williams, *Rethinking Gnosticism*) even proposes that because of Gnosticism's diversity there really is no Gnosticism! More troubling is the way that the diversity of modern interpretations of Gnosticism has contributed to a confusion of definitions, in which all precision and meaning seem to dissolve. The late and lamented Ioan Culianu (who was one of the most promising scholars in the field) wrote in a European publication:

> Once I believed that Gnosticism was a well-defined phenomenon belonging to the religious history of Late Antiquity. Of course, I was ready to accept the idea of different prolongations of ancient Gnosis, and even that of spontaneous generation of views of the world in which, at different times, the distinctive features of Gnosticism occur again.
>
> I was soon to learn however, that I was a naif indeed. Not only Gnosis was gnostic, but the Catholic authors were gnostic, the

Neoplatonic too, Reformation was gnostic, Communism was gnostic, Nazism was gnostic, liberalism, existentialism and psychoanalysis were gnostic too, modern biology was gnostic, Blake, Yeats, Kafka were gnostic. . . . I learned further that science is gnostic and superstition is gnostic . . . Hegel is gnostic and Marx is gnostic; all things and their opposite are equally gnostic. (Jacob Taubes, ed., *Gnosis und Politik* 290)

One important circumstance relating to this statement is widely overlooked in America. In Europe, the terms *Gnosis* and *Gnosticism* are almost always used interchangeably. The suggestion that the term *gnosis* ought to describe a state of consciousness while *Gnosticism* should denote the Gnostic system has never caught on. The use of the classical definition of *Gnosticism* persists in European literature, including the writings of recent scholars such as Gilles Quispel, Kurt Rudolph, and Giovanni Filoramo. The late Robert McLachlan put forth a proposal to distinguish between these terms, but current usage in Europe has not followed it. A word used in such contradictory ways may lose its meaning. No wonder the insightful writer Charles Coulombe despairs over the situation:

In reality, "Gnosticism," like "Protestantism," is a word that has lost most of its meaning. Just as we would need to know whether a "Protestant" writer is Calvinist, Lutheran, Anabaptist, or whatever in order to evaluate him properly, so too the "Gnostic" must be identified. (*New Oxford Review*, November 1991, 28–29)

POLITICAL CONFUSIONS, TRADITIONALIST FANTASIES, AND ACADEMIC AMBIGUITIES

One of the most confusing voices on Gnosticism comes from the discipline of political science. In his Walgreen Lectures at the University of Chicago in 1951, émigré scholar Eric Voegelin rose to the defense of what he called the "classic and Christian tradition" against what he perceived as the "growth of Gnosticism." He followed this opening salvo with several books *(The New Science of Politics*, the multivolume *Order and History*, and *Science, Politics, and Gnosticism)* and became a prophet of a new theory of history in which Gnosticism plays a nefarious role. All modern totalitarian ideologies are in some way spiritually related to Gnosticism, says Voegelin. Marxists, Nazis, and just about everybody else whom the good professor finds reprehensible are in reality Gnostics, engaged in "immanentizing the eschaton" by reconstituting society into a heaven on earth. Since Gnostics do not accept the conventional Christian eschaton of heaven and hell, Voegelin concludes that they must be engaged in a millenarian revolutionizing of earthly existence. At the same time, Voegelin has to admit that the Gnostics regard the earthly realm as unredeemably flawed. One wonders how such a realm could be turned into an earthly utopia. That Voegelin's supposed Gnostics have no knowledge of or sympathy with historical Gnosticism does not bother him either. Gnostics they are, and that is that.

The confusion Voegelin created was made worse by a number of conservative political thinkers, mainly those with Catholic connections. Thomas Molnar, Tilo Schabert, and Steven A. McKnight followed Voegelin's theories despite the obvious inconsistencies. In Molnar's view, Gnostics are responsible not only for all modern utopianism but also for modern people's inordinate attachment to science and technology. The scientific worldview, say these folk, is in fact a Gnostic worldview, and it is responsible for treating humans as machines and for making societies into machinelike collectives.

The politicized view of Gnosticism continues to have its adherents, but these are increasingly recruited from the lunatic fringe. Gnostics are still represented as dangerous subversives in pulp magazines and obscure conspiracy pamphlets "exposing" Freemasons, Satanists, and other pests. Meanwhile, respectable conservative thinkers have dropped the Gnostic issue. Some, like scholar and former U.S. senator S. I. Hayakawa, have subjected Voegelin and his theories to severe criticism and ridicule.

Other voices that cause confusion belong to writers bent on proving that within the existing major religions are secret traditions of gnosis that are not identical with the "heretical" Gnosticism of the early Christian centuries. In his 1947 work *The Perennial Philosophy,* Aldous Huxley promulgates a kind of gnosis that was, in effect, a mystery reserved for the elite, revealed at the dawn of history and handed down through various religious traditions, where it remains in spite of its ostensible incompatibility with the official dogmas of those traditions. Huxley's view approximates the more radical position held by Traditionalists such as René Guénon and Frithjof Schuon. (Part of Guénon's background that his followers tend to conceal is a period he spent as a bishop in the Gnostic Church of France and as a prominent Freemason and esotericist. He turned his back on not only Gnosticism but also Christianity when he converted to Sunni Islam.)

Huxley never passes judgment on anyone who calls himself a Gnostic. One only wishes the same could be said of other Traditionalists. Followers of Guénon often castigate the early Gnostic teachers in a manner reminiscent of ancient polemicists like Irenaeus. The Traditionalists' division of early Gnostic writers into "false Gnostics" and "authentic Gnostics" reflects standards that are nothing if not arbitrary; contemporary research indicates that, during the first three or four centuries after Christ, there was as yet no true orthodoxy and thus no heresy either. Instead, many religious teachings, including Gnosticism, flourished side by side. Certainly there were disagreements, but to arbitrarily extrapolate standards of falsity and authenticity from these polemics does not seem justified.

The 1988 edition of *The Nag Hammadi Library* contains a lengthy afterword entitled "The Modern Relevance of Gnosticism." Its author, Richard Smith, reviews the numerous developments in Western culture that appear related to Gnosticism. One would hope that here at last we might find a true definition of Gnosticism and a list of modern writers and thinkers who might appear as its representatives. Unfortunately, this is not the case.

Smith lists a number of important figures from the eighteenth century onward who were sympathetic to Gnosticism. He seems to be suggesting, however, that few of these thinkers had an adequate definition of Gnosticism, and so they more often than not misused and misappropriated the term. Smith accuses the eighteenth-century historian Edward Gibbon, for example, of a "mischievous lie" in referring to the Gnostics in complimentary terms. (Obviously Gibbon did not concur with the low esteem in which the church fathers had held Gnostics, but does this make him a liar?) And the Gnostic and Manichaean sympathies of Voltaire are represented as motivated solely by his opposition to churchly authority. But could the great philosopher have had other reasons for his views? It is well-known that Voltaire was an ardent Freemason; he might have gathered favorable information about Gnostics through the esoteric currents flowing in the secret fraternities of his time. Maybe he was privy to knowledge unknown to Smith. In the same vein, Smith implies that Jung appropriated Gnosticism by turning it into psychological theory: "Jung takes the entire dualist myth and locates it within the psyche," Smith writes.

Such accusations are critiqued in chapter 1. Ironically, among the criticisms directed against Voltaire, Jung, and others, Smith does not provide what he considers the true definition of Gnosticism. Gibbon was wrong, Voltaire and Jung were wrong, but who was right? We find no answer to such a question.

Fortunately, there are also a number of informed and fair-minded voices among writers on Gnosticism. The Italian scholar Giovanni Filoramo (*A History of Gnosticism* xiv) calls attention to the fact that the Nag Hammadi scriptures were favorably received by a wide public, in part because "certain areas of the cultural panorama showed a disposition, a peculiar sensitivity to the texts, which dealt with a phenomenon that they themselves had in some way helped to keep alive."

One of the persons who has kept the Gnostic phenomenon alive is Jung's close associate, the Gnostic scholar Gilles Quispel, who labored long and hard on relating the ancient Gnosis of Valentinus and other teachers to the modern gnosis of analytical psychology. He saw that the Gnostic effort involved deep insight into the ontological self and thus is analogous to the best in depth psychology. Quispel's major work on the subject, *Gnosis als Weltreligion* (1972), explains in detail the relationship of Jung's model to Gnostic teachings. Quispel, like Jung himself, did not reduce Gnostic teachings to depth psychology, but rather pointed to depth psychology as a key to understanding Gnosticism.

Another key figure in the reevaluation of ancient Gnosticism is Hans Jonas. A pupil of existentialist philosopher Martin Heidegger in the 1930s, Jonas turned his attention to the wisdom of the Gnostics and discovered in them an ancient relative of existential philosophy. Existentialism's pessimism regarding earthly life and its high regard for experience as opposed to theory thus found a forebear and analogue. Although critical of the Gnostics' "nihilism," Jonas was one of the most important figures, along with Jung, in bringing Gnostic teachings into modern perspective. His book *The Gnostic Religion* remains one of the great classics in this field.

The linkage effected by Quispel and Jonas between the Gnosticism of the past and living philosophies of the present was of crucial importance and came very close to supplying gnosis and Gnosticism with vital, living definitions. The questions posed—and answered—by the ancient Gnostics revealed their attitudes to be not outlandish and bizarre, but earlier discussions of issues addressed in more recent times by Freud, Jung, Kierkegaard, Heidegger, and many others.

TOWARD DEFINITION

The search for definitions is never easy, particularly in the social sciences. In these disciplines much attention must be given to the historical context in which beliefs and actions unfold. Crucial differences and similarities in nuance, tone, and subtlety of mood are more important here than hard and fast definitions. The debate about Gnosticism, it would seem, turns on such fine points, and it may well be that not much can be resolved by a definition. Nevertheless, the present chaos surrounding definitions of Gnosticism warrants an attempt.

To understand Gnosticism, writes Hans Jonas, one needs something very much like a musical ear. This kind of inner sensitivity is indeed more important than any set of definitions could ever be. Still, the nature of the ego-involved mind requires definitions and is uneasy without them. Real gnosis, of course, is not concerned with definitions. It is only when the impact of the Gnostic experience fades that one might even consider the task. The great translator G. R. S. Mead said it well when he wrote: "The illuminated soul that quits its prisonhouse, to bathe in the light of infinitude, can only recollect flashes of the Vision Glorious once it returns again to earth" (*Simon Magus* 49). The following itemized summary of Gnostic recognitions should therefore be viewed as a compendium of such "flashes of the Vision Glorious" rather than as a statement of religious tenets in the conventional mode:

1. There is an original and transcendental spiritual unity from which emanated a vast manifestation of pluralities.

2. The manifest universe of matter and mind was created not by the original spiritual unity but by spiritual beings possessing inferior powers.

3. One of the objectives of these creators is the perpetual separation of humans from the unity (God).

4. The human being is a composite: the outer aspect is the handiwork of the inferior creators, while the inner aspect is a fallen spark of the ultimate divine unity.

5. The sparks of transcendental holiness slumber in their material and mental prison, their self-awareness stupefied by the forces of materiality and mind.

6. The slumbering sparks have not been abandoned by the ultimate unity; rather, a constant effort directed toward their awakening and liberation comes forth from this unity.

7. The awakening of the inmost divine essence in humans comes through salvific knowledge, called "gnosis."

8. Gnosis is not brought about by belief or by the performance of virtuous deeds or by obedience to commandments; these at best serve to prepare one for liberating knowledge.

9. Among those aiding the slumbering sparks, a particular position of honor and importance belongs to a feminine emanation of the unity, Sophia (Wisdom). She was involved in the creation of the world and ever since has remained the guide of her orphaned human children.

10. From the earliest times of history, messengers of Light have been sent forth from the ultimate unity for the purpose of advancing gnosis in the souls of humans.

11. The greatest of these messengers in our historical and geographical matrix was the descended Logos of God manifest in Jesus Christ.

12. Jesus exercised a twofold ministry: he was a teacher, imparting instruction concerning the way of gnosis; and he was a hierophant, imparting mysteries.

13. The mysteries imparted by Jesus (which are also known as sacraments) are mighty aids toward gnosis and have been entrusted by him to his apostles and their successors.

14. Through the spiritual practice of the mysteries (sacraments) and a relentless and uncompromising striving for gnosis, humans can steadily advance toward liberation from all confinement, material and otherwise. The ultimate objective of this process of liberation is the achievement of salvific knowledge and with it, freedom from embodied existence and return to the ultimate unity.

Noted sociologist Max Weber wrote in *The Protestant Ethic and the Spirit of Capitalism* that "the perfect conceptual definition cannot stand at the beginning, but must be left until the end of the inquiry." It is therefore fitting that we consider this definition toward the end of this inquiry. Whether these points can aspire to anything like Weber's "perfect conceptual definition" is questionable. Still, they are in general historically accurate and terminologically definite, which is more than much of the current literature, academic or popular, offers. Distinctions like "orthodox gnosis" and "apostolic gnosis" have been avoided here, as well as categories like "false Gnostics" and "authentic Gnostics." Such judgments are made on the basis of orthodoxies that were never relevant to Gnostics or to Gnosticism.

Certainly, the fourteen points offered here have all been part of the Gnostic tradition and have been espoused by Gnostics at one time or another. At least the first ten of the fourteen points may be considered wholly authoritative, even in a non-Christian Gnostic sense, and thus the absence of any of them from a person's worldview might disqualify him or her as a Gnostic. Gnostics, when they stand up to identify themselves, would have to agree to the majority of these tenets, but whether the interpretation of them would be literal, psychological, philosophical, or other must be left to the individual.

At least, we may no longer have to quote *Through the Looking-Glass* (ch. 6) regarding the definition of Gnosticism:

> "When *I* use a word," Humpty Dumpty said, . . . "it means just what I choose it to mean—neither more nor less."
> "The question is," said Alice, "whether you *can* make words mean so many different things."

GNOSTIC LITERATURE:
MYTH, TRUTH, AND NARRATIVE

Religion has always been a source of creativity and imagination. The psychological and/or metaphysical forces that account for religious experience and revelation are closely related to the wellspring from which poetry, drama, and other forms of secular literature flow. The Christian Bible has inspired much art, yet at the same time Christian orthodoxy, with its insistence on the literalness and factuality of its sacred literature, has also hindered the conjunction of religious and artistic creativity.

The developments that stifled much imaginative creativity within Christianity were largely connected with the suppression of Gnosticism. Gnostics were practitioners par excellence of symbolism, allegory, metaphor, myth, and creative ambiguity when it came to their literary works. As pointed out earlier, these works were more often than not the result of nonordinary states of consciousness experienced by Gnostic sages. Numerous researchers have noted that experiences gained in nonordinary states have affinities with myth, poetry, and symbol. By contrast, in the orthodox Christian view, which is more prosaic, a good Christian ought to have dogmas to believe in and commandments to observe and not much more. Sophisticated literary devices, such as the Gnostics used, were not very suitable to the orthodox objectives; neither was visionary literature. Notably, the Protestant reformers outdid the earlier orthodox church fathers in this regard; they excised the most poetic portions of the Bible and declared them apocryphal. (Luther even wanted to remove the Book of Revelation from the Bible, because of its symbolic, visionary character.)

Myth and metaphor were of course present in the literature of pagan Greece and Rome. (The relatively hostile attitude of many orthodox Christians toward myths was largely because of their rejection of the pagan mind-set.) Yet despite its grandeur, the literature of the Homeric myths lacks something that is present in the writings of the Gnostics. Julian Jaynes points out that much of the mythological literature of ancient Greece lacks subjective consciousness and self-reflection. Karl Kerényi, perhaps one of the most insightful modern scholars of mythology, states that the myths of the Neoplatonists and of the Gnostics are much closer to the mystical experience from which they were derived than are the Homeric myths *(Essays on a Science of Mythology)*. Such recognitions show us that not all myths are equal; some are more revelatory than others.

In addition to its mystical authenticity, Gnostic literature brings certain themes into Western thought. Some of these are human forlornness, homesickness, alienation, entrapment within a tyrannical cosmic system, and the possibility of ultimate freedom—not only from political, economic, or ideological oppression, but from the human existential condition itself. Once such themes appeared in Western thought and literature, they became an intrinsic part of its heritage, never to be forgotten again.

SCRAPS FROM THE GNOSTIC TABLE

"The Gnosis, according to Its Foes" is the title G. R. S. Mead gave to the heresiologist church fathers' writings on Gnosticism (in *Fragments of a Faith Forgotten*). This literature presents many challenges—principally of annoyance—to the reader. Still, for many centuries this was the only available literature having to do with Gnosticism. Three of the writers were known for their vehemently anti-Gnostic views: Irenaeus of Lyons, Hippolytus of Rome, and Epiphanius of Salamis. All three were elevated to sainthood, and the works of all three are never free from mendacity and theological ire. Their writings have to be read with skeptical caution, especially when their polemical intent becomes apparent.

On the other hand, these works are valuable for their quotations and summaries of Gnostic teachings. There is relatively little doubt about the substantive accuracy of these quotations and summaries. At the same time, we must remember that they are recorded by avowed opponents of Gnosticism; it is difficult to trust the fairness of writers who openly regard their subject as wrong and deceitful, the very spawn of Satan. Two other writers are of a far more honorable character and are, in fact, fairly close to the Gnostics in some of their thinking: these are Clement of Alexandria and Origen of Alexandria. Clement, particularly, uses the word *gnosis* frequently and regards gnosis as an approach to religion that is superior to mere faith.

In a different category of literature belong the so-called Apostolic Acts, most of which were probably written by Gnostic authors, especially Leucius Charinus, as discussed in chapter 8. These books enjoyed great popularity throughout the early Christian centuries and were hardly regarded as heterodox at all. The most important from a Gnostic point of view are the Acts of John and the Acts of Thomas, since the Gnostic element is still very evident in them.

One of the finest examples of Gnostic symbolic allegory is a portion of the Acts of Thomas called the "Hymn of the Pearl," or the "Hymn of the Robe of Glory." It is a poetic first-person narrative said to have been composed by the apostle Thomas. The poem has been expertly translated by Mead and is available in other translations as well. It describes in allegorical form the monomyth of Gnosticism: the journey of the human spirit from the Fullness to embodiment on the earth and back to the Fullness again. The work is in some ways reminiscent of the story of the prodigal son, although its style is far more poetic and its content more archetypal. The meaning seems to be multileveled, allowing persons with various degrees of gnosis to profit from reading it. The protagonist fits the category that some modern mythologists call the "redeemed redeemer," for he comes to this earth to liberate and retrieve the pearl (an obvious symbol for a Gnostic Light Treasure—perhaps the divine sparks in earthly captivity), and in his attempt he falls prey to forgetfulness and alienation himself. Awakened by a letter from the Fullness, he proceeds with his redemptive work and eventually returns to the realm of his celestial parents.

The Acts of John contains several striking chapters on the actions of Jesus just prior to his crucifixion, as well as on the crucifixion itself. The portion usually translated as the "Hymn of Jesus" is particularly fascinating. The hymn is a poem of undoubted Gnostic content that, as noted in chapter 7, is sung by Jesus and the apostles while they perform a mystic dance on the night of Maundy Thursday. Sacred dances are notably absent from Christian ritual, and to the orthodox mind the image of Jesus dancing may appear sacrilegious even today. The Ethiopian Coptic Church, however, does include a sacred dance in its Eucharist. Who is to say whether this might not be a remnant of Coptic Gnostic practice, similar to the one described in the "Hymn of Jesus"?

Beginning in the late eighteenth century, three collections of original Gnostic writings appeared in various institutions in England and Europe. How they managed to remain concealed for some sixteen hundred years and then suddenly made their appearance is one of history's mysteries. In 1784, among the possessions of a British physician named Askew was discovered an archaic book of 346 pages. It was acquired by the British Museum and named the Askew Codex. Its contents are written in the Sahidic dialect of Coptic, which might indicate that it comes from Upper Egypt, where the famous Nag Hammadi writings were discovered in the twentieth century. The main text of the Askew Codex, the Pistis Sophia, tells the story of the Gnostic feminine wisdom figure. The narrator is Jesus himself. To this day this work is our major source for the story of the fall and redemption of Sophia (see chapter 4).

The codex was slow to be translated or commented upon, but by the late nineteenth century it had attracted the attention of Mead, who prepared the first accessible translation of the Pistis Sophia in fine English prose. The redoubtable Madame Blavatsky, Mead's mentor, encouraged him in this task and just before her death wrote some commentaries on the text, including a diagram that she drew to illustrate its contents. Mead's translation remains the most generally available and insightfully prepared rendition of this work and has been commented upon with admiration by many, including Jung.

Of more complex content and also of great interest is the Bruce Codex, which was discovered in the Middle East by the Scottish traveler James Bruce and deposited by him in the Bodleian Library at Oxford. This book consists of two parts, the larger being The Gnosis of the Invisible God or The Books of Jeu, and the smaller, The Untitled Apocalypse. As noted in chapter 7, the former recounts an amazing visionary journey in which Jesus takes his disciples into the inner worlds and bestows spiritual initiations on them. The text is filled with diagrams and magical sigils accompanied by verbal formulas that are either in an unknown tongue, or represent examples of "glossolalia" (speaking in tongues). The treatise was puzzling to earlier scholars and at times has been derisively called magical. Happily, more positive attention has been given to it in recent times. Regrettably, however, in none of the English editions are the translation and the reproductions of the designs exact.

The Untitled Apocalypse has been translated and commented upon by scholars more often than The Books of Jeu. This treatise, which is also called The Gnosis of the Light, is a mystical work of sublime grandeur and beauty describing the stage-by-stage unfoldment of manifesting Divinity and also the mission of the spark of divine Light in the world.

The third of the trio of Gnostic codices that surfaced in the nineteenth century is the Berlin Codex, also known, because of its place of origin in Egypt, as the Akhmim Codex. Although the illustrious German scholar Carl Schmidt prepared translations of portions of this codex, the contents were not published for a very long time. It consists of three tractates, the most famous of which is The Gospel of Mary, which concerns a narrative of mystical actions and teachings of Jesus as recounted by Mary Magdalene. This treatise has been published in English in the last portion of *The Nag Hammadi Library in English* and thus is generally available. It is one of the major Gnostic works concerned with Mary Magdalene; its mystical tone and curious, at times sexual, symbolism should render it of interest for contemporary study and comment. The other treatises, the Acts of Peter and The Wisdom of Jesus Christ (as it was once known) are in need of further exploration also.

The appearance of original Gnostic writings transformed both academic Gnostic studies and popular interest in Gnosticism in the late nineteenth century and through the first half of the twentieth century. The Pistis Sophia, in particular, created a considerable sensation in circles of esoteric spirituality. The emerging Gnostic revival of that period would have been unthinkable but for these discoveries. Since the beginning of the twentieth century, Gnosticism has been at least sporadically an object of moderate public interest. Novels, poems, and particularly Theosophical and other esoteric literature have contained more and more references to Gnosticism. Esoteric teachers, like Rudolf Steiner, George I. Gurdjieff, and P. D. Ouspensky, have availed themselves of Gnostic thought. The scene was then ready for a major infusion of Gnostic wisdom, which appeared at the halfway point of the century in the form of the most important discovery of Gnostic writings ever: the Nag Hammadi library.

NEW LIGHT FROM AN OLD CAVE: THE NAG HAMMADI SCRIPTURES

Until the end of World War II, Gnostic texts were limited to the summaries and recensions of Gnostic teachings written by the church fathers named earlier and the three original Gnostic codices just discussed. It is to their credit that so many insightful students of the Gnostic tradition, including Mead and Jung, managed to form a fairly accurate picture of Gnosticism on the basis of such scanty evidence. Supplementing their reading with their own gnosis, many of these modern Gnostics understood the meaning of these often labyrinthine texts very well. What this proves is that to understand a Gnostic text one should be a Gnostic. Writers like Mead and Jung wrote about Gnosticism from the inside, as it were, and this explains their remarkable grasp of their subject.

The year 1945 brought an astounding event that changed the face of Gnostic studies forever. In December of that year, an Arab peasant discovered a clay vessel filled with manuscripts while digging for fertilizer in a valley in Upper Egypt. The exact location of the find has remained a matter of speculation. Some suspect that the discovery was really made in one of the many caves found in the mountain range that overlooks the Nag Hammadi valley, for it was in this area that the founder of Christian monasticism, the Coptic monk Pachomius, had established his large monastic community. Very likely the thirteen papyrus codices that comprise what has been named the Nag Hammadi Library constituted some of the less orthodox reading material of the monks at this monastery. When in the fourth century a wave of religious persecution swept through Egypt, the anxious monks may have decided to bury their heretical books. Little did they know that their library would not surface for sixteen hundred years.

Years after the find, the discoverer reported that for a while he had been reluctant to open the large earthenware jar for fear that it might contain a *jinn* (spirit). When he eventually broke the red jar with his mallet, a cloud of golden dust rose and dissipated into the desert air. Perhaps a certain "genie" was now indeed out of the bottle and would cause strange developments for years to come.

Much academic and political wrangling has accompanied the translation and publication of the Nag Hammadi Library. Political upheavals in Egypt led to the expelling of Western scholars, and the find languished in obscurity. One codex—containing among other tractates the famous Gospel of Truth, possibly authored by Valentinus—was spirited out of Egypt and discovered at a bookseller's shop by Jung's Gnostic expert, Quispel. Jung's friends secured the purchase price and presented the codex to Jung on the occasion of his eightieth birthday. The aged Gnostic master of Zurich, greatly moved by the gift, was very interested in seeing the rest of the Library translated and published.

(The present author has been accused of exaggerating Jung's role in the publication of the Nag Hammadi Library. The truth of the matter is that while the practical project of rescuing the find and translating its content was largely the work of Dr. James Robinson of the Institute of Antiquity and Christianity in Claremont, California, Jung's vital interest in the Gnostic documents facilitated the publication psychologically. Jung's endorsement of the importance of these writings contributed to the widespread positive response to the publication project. The influence of someone with the stature of Jung, who knew Gnosticism from the inside, as it were, cannot be exaggerated.)

The Nag Hammadi Library is just what its name declares: a library. It is not a canonical collection of sacred texts but a library containing diverse reading materials of Gnostic interest. A few of the tractates contain writings that are not strictly speaking Gnostic, for instance, the *Zostrianos,* a portion of Plato's *Republic,* and the splendid Hermetic initiation discourse The Eighth Reveals the Ninth. The rest of the considerable material may be classified under six main headings. The first of these concerns creative and redemptive mythology, giving accounts of the creation of the world, of Adam and Eve, and of the descent of the redeeming Logos as Jesus. Many of the passages quoted in chapter 3 are from this source. A second category consists of commentaries and observations on various Gnostic themes, such as the nature of the soul, spiritual salvation, and the relationship of the soul to the world. The most noteworthy of these treatises is the Gospel of Truth, contained in the Jung Codex, which consists of a beautiful discourse concerning the mission of the savior and of his spiritual message. The third category contains liturgical and initiatory texts, of which The Eighth Reveals the Ninth is the most fascinating. The fourth category consists of writings concerning the divine feminine, particularly Sophia. The fifth group includes writings about some of the apostles. The sixth category contains sayings of Jesus as well as incidents in his life.

There are only four scriptures in the Nag Hammadi collection that bear the title "gospel": the Gospel according to Thomas, the Gospel of Philip, the Gospel of Truth, and the Gospel of the Egyptians. Of these, certainly the *Gospel according to Thomas* is the most accessible and therefore the most popular. Unlike the four canonical Gospels, it is not a narrative describing Jesus' life. Rather, it is a collection of Jesus' sayings. Some of these are virtually identical with those found in canonical sources, while many others are distinctly Gnostic in character. Certainly a Gnostic note is struck in the introductory sayings:

These are the secret words which the living Jesus spoke. Whoever finds the interpretation of these words will not taste death.

And he [Jesus] said: Let him who seeks keep seeking until he finds. And when he finds he will be troubled; when he becomes troubled he will marvel, and when he has marveled he will rule over the all. (prologue and saying 1)

Note that there is no exhortation to belief, no statement that if people believe they will be saved. Instead, the reader is enjoined to interpret, understand, seek, and become a master over the all. These are prescriptions for Gnostic rather than orthodox salvation. Gnosis as self-knowledge is clearly emphasized:

When you come to know yourselves, then you will become known, and you will know that you are the children of the Living Father. But when you will not know yourselves, then you will be in poverty and you yourselves will be the poverty. (saying 3)

What modern depth psychologist could disagree with the following?

If you bring forth that which is within your selves, what you bring forth will save you. If you do not bring forth what is within you, what you do not bring forth will kill you. (saying 70)

Some of the Nag Hammadi scriptures contain clear indications of the much criticized "elitism" of the Gnostics. The treatise entitled The Apocalypse of Peter contains an interesting passage in which Jesus is laughing and glad (as he is in the account in the Acts of John) while being crucified. Peter is dismayed that the crowd cannot see the true nature of Jesus' crucifixion and says to Jesus: "Lord, no one is looking at thee"; to which Jesus replies: "I have told you: Leave the blind alone." That is, the majority is always blind. To try to explain to the blind what they are constitutionally incapable of seeing is a waste of time and effort. The hidden meaning of events, teachings, and indeed of life is known only to the few. Such sayings stand in powerful contrast to the orthodox contention that Jesus revealed everything. Hendrik Ibsen in his splendid drama *The Enemy of the People* makes his hero exclaim: "The majority? The majority is never right!" The Gnostics would agree.

A professor of religious studies reported in the 1970s that after having recommended to one of his students that he read the Gospel according to Thomas, the student joyously reported to the class: "Jesus is a Zen Buddhist." Indeed, the intent of many of the sayings of Jesus found in the Gnostic scriptures seems similar to that of Zen koans. They are not so much designed to convey information as they are calculated to cause spiritual transformation in the disciple.

It is sometimes alleged that the Gnostic Gospels lack the emphasis on love that is found in the canonical Gospel message. It is presumed by the critics that the Jesus appearing in these gospels is not the concerned miracle worker who in his pity for humans raises the dead, heals the ailing, and makes the sightless see again. But this reasoning is false. The Jesus who emerges from the Gospel according to Thomas and similar scriptures is a spiritual teacher, a guide of souls, who initiates the qualified elect into gnosis. Like Gautama the Buddha before him, he recognizes that to physically alleviate suffering is not enough, for the ultimate roots of suffering reside in the mind and heart. As in the canonical Gospels, so also in the Gnostic Gospels he advises his disciples to love one another:

> Love your brother as your soul; keep him as the apple of your eye. (saying 25)

But as for every Gnostic, so for Jesus also: the most effective act of love is spiritual liberation, which brings the cessation of all physical and psychic suffering as well. For this reason, the Jesus of these gospels will never be a suitable figure for the liberation theologians; the liberation he brings is not political or economic but spiritual. But—and this should certainly not be forgotten—because it is a liberation that liberates *from* the world rather than *in* the world, it is also a liberation that is final. And that is certainly worth a great deal.

Always and everywhere in the Nag Hammadi collection of scriptures, we find the typically Gnostic conjunction between the self and the transcendental nonself—the indwelling spirit and the Godhead beyond the aeons. The way to the Divine is through oneself. The Nag Hammadi treatise The Teachings of Silvanus expresses this clearly:

> Enlighten your mind. . . . Light the lamp within you. Knock on yourself as upon a door and walk upon yourself as on a straight road. For if you walk on the road, it is impossible for you to go astray. . . . Open the door for you so that you may know what it is.

The Nag Hammadi codices are a magnificent storehouse of Gnostic wisdom. Not only are they the largest collection of Gnostic writings ever discovered, but through their discovery the volume of available Gnostic lore has multiplied manifold. For the first time in two thousand years, there is sufficient Gnostic material to persuade a growing number of worthy persons in our culture that a reevaluation of

Christendom's judgment of the Gnostics might be in order. We can see that the picture drawn for us long ago concerning the early beginnings of Christianity was gravely flawed. There was no single "great church," no pristine orthodox religious institution from which the "Gnostic heresy" willfully and perversely split off. Rather, Christendom was split from the beginning; it was a gathering of many kinds of belief and interpretation and many kinds of gnosis as well. Today, when non-Gnostic Christianity is again split into hundreds of divisions, there might be a place again for the falsely accused and shunned "heretic," the Gnostic. The picture is changing, and the agent of change has come to us from the sands of the desert, from the old red earthenware jar that released more than just a small cloud of golden dust in 1945.

In consequence of the diligent and devoted work of many scholars, the entire Nag Hammadi Library has been available in easy English prose at popular prices since 1977. Never before in history has so much fuel for the study and assimilation of these teachings been available. In an otherwise confused and painfully divided world, these are good signs indeed.

Mead, one of the greatest of the early workers in the vineyard of Gnostic scriptures, wrote nearly a hundred years ago but with a sense of perennial timeliness:

> It is true that today we speak openly of many things that the Gnostic wrapped up in symbol and myth; nevertheless our real knowledge on such subjects is not so very far in advance of the great doctors of the Gnosis as we are inclined to imagine; now, as then, there are only a few who really know what they are writing about, while the rest copy, compare, adapt, and speculate. . . .
>
> Who knows with the intellect enough to decide on all these high subjects for his fellows? Let each follow the Light as he sees it—there is enough for all; so that at last we may see "all things turned into Light—sweet joyous Light." (*Fragments of a Faith Forgotten* 592, 606–7)

CHAPTER FOURTEEN

GNOSTICISM AND
POSTMODERN THOUGHT

Gnosticism strikes us as both anciently remote and vitally contemporary. This may be partly due to a certain similarity in the historical settings of ancient Gnosticism on the one hand and of the postmodern thought world on the other. The milieus of the early centuries of the Christian era and the twentieth and possibly twenty-first centuries are not as different as one might expect. Both eras boast evidence of relentless material progress. The Pax Americana, like the Pax Romana, has brought a measure of stability, security, and prosperity in its wake. (The markets of second-century Alexandria served purposes similar to those of our shopping malls.) Yet both periods are also replete with cruelty, anxiety, and sorrow. Rome was built on the labor of slaves and on the blood of conquered peoples; the late-modern and postmodern world is one in which extermination camps, totalitarian tyranny, and terrorist attacks have come to flourish. Gnostics and their spiritual kith and kin in both periods are those who have concluded that the great secret of life cannot be found in such a world,

205

and thus it must be searched for in deeper and less mundane sources.

The homespun, virtuous cultural ambience of the Roman republic gave way to the multicultural, grandiosely nihilistic spirit of the Roman Empire; so also, the optimistic, secular, rationalist, and progressive foundations of modern Western society are currently dissolving. Not so long ago we generally assumed that through reason we would discover the "laws of nature" and that through the application of these laws things would get better and better. Today this assumption is rarely unquestioned. The promise of progress through reason is not taken seriously by many.

At the time of the Gnostics, it was the Olympian throng of the old classical gods that failed. In our own time, we have seen the twilight of the modern gods—political ideology, science, sociology, medical-based psychology, and most recently perhaps environmentalism. Our culture still functions as if founded on the rationalistic humanism of the eighteenth-century Enlightenment, but it does so with less and less confidence in that philosophy. New doubts are eroding the secular faith of the last three hundred years. Nature, once viewed as inherently orderly, is coming to be viewed by some scientists as far more disorderly than anyone imagined. Human history, also, is no longer seen as something that rational humanity can bend to its liking. Increasingly, the historical process is being seen as a force unto itself, not amenable to the dictates of human reason and purposes. And encompassing all, the universe itself is frequently seen not as the harmonious cosmos of old but, with the emergence of chaos theory, as a phenomenon of constant flux and flow where most of the portentous phenomena are inherently unpredictable. Donald Worster, a scholarly analyst of the new theories and an internationally recognized environmental historian, has written: "Ours is a postmodernist post-structuralist age, when all that has seemed solid melts into air" (interview in the *Wall Street Journal*, July 11, 1994).

To illustrate the situation in down-to-earth terms: Consider the changes in such cultural hallmarks as the themes played out on the motion picture screen. The movies of the 1950s, with notable exceptions, showed us a world happily progressing through the efforts of science. Four decades later, *Jurassic Park* introduced us to a terrifying natural world, overrun by forces unleashed by an irresponsible and venal science. Are the differences in these two portrayals coincidental? The more keen observers don't think so. They find that the differences mark the raising of anxious questions about human behavior and moral values.

The postmodernist trend, which has proved so destructive to the old, confident faith in orderly progress, itself originates in scientific thought. Chaos theory has extended further some of the long-standing insights of scholars concerning the unpredictability of the universe and of nature—beginning with Heisenberg's "uncertainty principle" enunciated in the 1920s. In brief, the theory holds that the long-term behavior of systems (such as the weather, or the universe itself) cannot be predicted with certainty. To make a definite prediction requires knowing the initial conditions of the system to an absolute degree of accuracy. This is obviously impossible; therefore, the principle of random events appears to be more prevalent than the principle of predictability. These dramatic changes in scientific thought ultimately reflect a fundamental change in the larger culture. It is not only the citadel of science but also literature, theater, visual arts, and social sciences that have been invaded by the centripetal force of deconstructionism. Literature is being deconstructed along political and sociological trajectories, and the result is an erosion of the respect in which the literary heritage of the culture was traditionally held.

An ancient Gnostic would probably find chaos theory an exciting piece of news, since it suggests a look at reality similar to the Gnostic worldview. The cosmos being the design of the Demiurge, it is suspect in numerous ways—not the least of these being that it is chiefly counterfeit. For example, the Gnostic scriptures say that the Demiurge devised cycles of time as a poor imitation of timeless eternity. The orderliness, grandeur, and lawfulness of the cosmos are largely fake; and more than likely, underneath the veneer of unchanging order and causal progression the cosmos is chaotic and random. To Einstein's famous statement that God "does not play dice," the Gnostic might respond ironically, "Oh, doesn't he now?" IALDABAOTH, one of the most common names of the Demiurge, means "the childish god," and it certainly would be in keeping with the character of such a being to play dice with the universe he had cobbled together.

Gnostics of course distinguish between the God who fabricates the cosmos—and who may very well play dice—and the transcendent Godhead that exists beyond all worlds and systems. The transcendent God is less likely to play dice. Moreover, in the Gnostic way of thinking, categorical statements are rarely appropriate. Several Gnostic scriptures clearly indicate that aspects of the supreme Godhead have secretly penetrated the realm of the Demiurge. An implicit transcendental element underlies the false order of the cosmos—and thus underlies the chaos as well. The core concept here has to do with consciousness, or more precisely, with gnosis. When the cosmos is deconstructed, it reveals itself as chaos. But when the chaos is penetrated by the kind of altered consciousness known as gnosis, the chaos reveals an implicit reality that has its own order. This order is very different from the illusory order of the world of the Demiurge. To perceive chaos beneath the surface of cosmos thus may be a first step toward gnosis, but further steps are required. Chaos theory is discovered by rational, scientific means, while the transcendental order can be discovered only by gnosis. This order beyond order surfaces only in exalted, nonordinary states of consciousness. Mathematical calculations and literary deconstruction will not disclose this reality, but gnosis will.

GNOSIS AND NIHILISM

Chaos theory and its implications have struck terror in the hearts of many observers. Donald Worster asks in an interview, "What is there to love or preserve in a universe of chaos? How are people supposed to behave in such a universe? If that is the kind of place we inhabit, why not go ahead with all our private ambitions, free of any fear that we may be doing special damage?" (*Wall Street Journal*, July 11, 1994).

Nearly two thousand years ago, critics asked similar questions of the Gnostics. The bone of contention at that time was the Gnostics' refusal to regard Mosaic law and other religious rules as necessary to salvation, or more correctly, to gnosis. To be sure, Gnostics did not hold that laws, religiously sanctioned or otherwise, were useless to society. What they protested was the notion that by "behaving well" in the world one could purchase admission to salvation and heavenly bliss. Still, the charge of antinomianism (opposition to the law) was consistently repeated against the Gnostics. In more recent times criticism changed into accusations of nihilism, meaning primarily moral nihilism.

With the passage of time, Western culture at large became less concerned with Mosaic law and more concerned with the order and lawfulness of the cosmos. To criticize the commandments of Moses was not reprehensible, but presumably in a lawful universe it was incumbent on people to behave in a law-abiding manner. With the apparent near collapse of the secular, rationalist faith of the culture, the fear of moral nihilism is certainly not without justification. When a philosophical vacuum begins to yawn in a culture, people will try to fill it in various ways. The selfish, the greedy, and the lustful—the hyletics of Gnostic lore—will use the opportunity to advance their own purposes. Others—whom the Gnostics might have called psychics—will seek refuge in the "old-time religion" of fundamentalism and retreat into a fortress of religious law. And the remaining, usually small, minority—the pneumatics, or persons of spirit—will respond by turning inward, toward liberating gnosis. It was thus in the days of the Roman empire, and it might be thus today.

But what of the charge of nihilism leveled against the Gnostics? This charge was first powerfully revived by Hans Jonas, a scholar otherwise sympathetic to Gnosticism, whose work on the subject has revolutionized Gnostic studies since the 1950s. Ethical monotheism, which is the core teaching of Judaism, and to a lesser extent of Zoroastrianism, Islam, and Christianity, has always had an overwhelming concern with the infusion of social rules with divine authority. The law must be obeyed because it is given by God, and if we do not obey, God will smite us in various ways.

The Gnostics of ancient times as well as of today cannot and will not go along with the dictum of ethical monotheism. The reasons are many. Mythically speaking, the source of the law is the Demiurge—a fact that diminishes the authority of the law, to say the least. Historically speaking, it is evident that Jesus, the latest and greatest messenger, has abrogated the old law of Moses and replaced it with his own, which Gnostics call the law of love. (The statement that he came "to fulfill the law" is interpreted by Gnostics as "completing" or "finishing" the law.) Lastly, the laws of society are regarded by Gnostics as a kind of secondary reality, a counterfeit of spiritual reality. People who are unwilling to rise to spiritual vision project transcendental reality upon institutions and their rules, sanctifying and empowering social laws as "divine rights." When humans allow law to become their primary religious focus, they cut themselves off from the possibility of gnosis. Gnostics, on the other hand, strive after the spirit, of which it has been written that "it bloweth where it listeth." The attitude of most mystics, including the greatest Kabbalists, Christian mystics, and Sufis, toward religious law generally mirrors this Gnostic disdain.

WHERE GNOSTICS DIFFER FROM MODERN
AND POSTMODERN NIHILISTS

Most recent critics of Gnosticism as moral nihilism have linked Gnostics with existentialism, with Nietzschean thinking, and at times even with German Nazi attitudes. Behind their criticism lurks the idea that people who pay no attention to the law of Moses are likely to condone all sorts of reprehensible behavior, and moreover, that if someone feels that the world is meaningless, such a person is bound to lead a life bereft of meaning. Similar arguments might be advanced against a good deal of postmodern thinking also.

Similarities, however, do not mean identities. Existentialism and other modern and postmodern teachings, including chaos theory, are similar to Gnosticism only in part. Modern and postmodern thought have emphasized, in a rather Gnostic way, such themes as alienation, forlornness, the soul's fall into the world—its captivity, its anxiety, and its existential terror. These recognitions, however, represent roughly one half of the Gnostic image of reality. Nowhere in existentialist and related thought do we find a firm commitment to an absolute reality beyond this world to which the alienated, anxious, dejected soul may journey. Modern and postmodern humanity is hopelessly unredeemed, while the Gnostic is filled with the hope of redemption. Furthermore, Gnosticism is a tradition replete with what generally characterizes a tradition: teachings, scriptures, and spiritual practices. Our age, being generally suspicious of tradition, naturally tends to emphasize the non-traditional side of Gnosticism. Yet it is its traditional side that, unlike so much of modern and postmodern thought, points the way to the destiny of human life. The Gnostic knows that humans had their origin in eternity and that they also have eternity as their goal. And this makes all the difference!

And what of the personal aspect of the charge of moral nihilism?

Ancient Gnostics were not noted as less law-abiding folk than mainstream Christians. If we discount some of the early accusations of sexual excess as politically motivated calumny, there is really nothing left that would implicate Gnostics as criminals or even as immoralists. It is well-known that the Manichaean Gnostics led lives of exceptional ascetic purity, and the same can be said of the medieval Cathars, of whom one of their theological foes, St. Bernard of Clairvaux, said that "their morals were the purest."

Certainly the mystical life, whether Gnostic or other, carries as much peril as promise, and some of the peril concerns the behavior of the mystic. Mysticism sometimes leads to fanaticism, as such phenomena as the Christian Crusades and the Inquisition, as well as the actions of the Islamic revolution in Iran, prove. Many a crusading monk or an inquisitor might qualify as a mystic of sorts, as would some cruel mullahs of today. It is to the credit of the practitioners of the Gnostic tradition that they avoided pitfalls of this nature.

If denial of the graven images of culture constitutes nihilism, then the Gnostic might justly plead guilty. Gnostics always maintained a certain basic honesty about life in the world. They refused to invest any society—were it Rome, the Persian empire, or the medieval Catholic Church, which they referred to as "the Beast"—with the positive projections that worshippers of institutions tend to employ. Yet the Gnostics were not anxious to be martyred. One of the church fathers' accusations against them was that they would evade martyrdom at the hands of the Roman persecutors of Christians. Even the Cathars, whose courage no one doubted, did not seek out death at the hands of the inquisitors, although when it became inevitable they accepted their lot with great dignity, walking into the flames singing. The Gnostic Gospel of Philip says ironically that even as God created man, so men return the favor by creating their own gods whom they worship. It would be better, says this scripture, for such gods to worship men! The implications are clear: the ideas, projections, and attachments that most people nourish are no more than lifeless graven images. To worship them is an exercise in utter futility.

Every age has its favorite idols. In the Middle Ages, it was the Christian ideal as interpreted by popes and bishops that was sacrosanct and to which all, even emperors, were subservient. In the age of science and humanism, the gospel of human progress became the sacred idol of the culture. Today, this idol is also tottering on its pedestal, largely due to postmodern ideas combined with the sorrowful lessons of history. If progress manifests in human history, why did we have to live through the most bloody and painful century of all, the twentieth? Were Hitler, Stalin, and Mao Tse-tung really the products of progress? Ought the victims of Hiroshima to be grateful for the blessing of progress that came to them in the form of the atom bomb? Biologist David Ehrenfeld (*The Arrogance of Humanism*) accuses progressivism and humanism of excessive hubris when he says, "The idea of progress is the disease of our time. In truth we are not inventing our future. We are just engineering changes whose outcomes we cannot predict and which often turn out to be terrible." The Gnostic would certainly agree.

If progress does not obtain on its own accord, is revolution better? If institutions refuse to change, should we invest our minds, hearts, and lives in changing them? Are we to forever storm the Bastilles of this world, hoping that each battle, each revolution and war, will be the last? There are no records of wars or revolutions willingly waged by Gnostics. Even when Cathar sympathizers reached for the sword in the Languedoc, they did so in self-defense and grudgingly. Gnostics were never as interested in changing the world as they were in transcending it.

It is indeed possible that the postmodern era, with its chaos theory and other preoccupations designed to deconstruct so many of the ideals as well as the idols of the culture, will bring an increase of nihilism in the world. Nihilism, after all, derives its name from the Latin word for "nothing." When everything is deconstructed, what is likely to remain is just that: nothing. Or is it? If in the midst of such changes there emerges a Gnostic hope, then the vanishing of earthly constructs may be followed by the return of the spirit to the Fullness. It is often thus—when the temporal is discredited, the eternal comes into its own. When humans become disillusioned—when their illusions are taken away—they may discover the real. In this respect, Gnostics are indeed optimists; they are confident that gnosis may come to those who awaken from the deep sleep of the world.

GNOSTIC PERSPECTIVES ON THE INFORMATION AGE

Postmodernity is inexorably intertwined with the concept as well as the reality of the information age. The scientists who conclude from their calculations that chaos may be more real than cosmos, and the literati and critics who are busily deconstructing literature and the social sciences, all do their work primarily by resorting to information appearing on the screens of their computers. To the extent that today's intellectual becomes aware of Gnosticism, he or she is likely to interpret gnosis as information. To this point, one of the most creative writers of imaginative literature, Philip K. Dick, who enthusiastically incorporated Gnosticism into several of his works, interpreted gnosis simply as "information." Yet is gnosis really no more than information? The high regard in which information is held in our day is undoubtedly due to the influence of the computer, which has become the prime instrument of information. A vast amount of information, as well as an equally vast amount of misinformation, pours into countless minds daily from the computer screen. Our newest gods are the data we evoke magically on the screen, which promises to connect us with all that is and possibly could be.

It is a truism that information is only as good as the source from which it is derived. A less frequently mentioned truth is that information is also only as good as the mind that receives it. In the age of information, the temptation to a certain cognitive arrogance, which is already well-developed in our culture, grows greater. Cognitive arrogance may be defined as the assumption that because one has access to information, one therefore knows what is true and helpful and needs no tradition or source of inspiration besides the conscious ego and its resources of data. In spiritual matters, such arrogance can be unfortunate indeed. A person might decide to pick and choose information of an allegedly spiritual nature in an attempt to synthesize his or her own unique stairway to heaven. The computer screen, or any source of information, becomes like a vast table in a cafeteria of ideas where one may graze in a "buffet-style" manner to one's ego's content.

In the information age, one frequently encounters the grandiloquent declaration: "I know what's best for me! I will choose what suits my unique requirements." This is tantamount to an ill person saying to a qualified physician: "I know my body. I will choose the remedies myself, without regard for your medical expertise." Or more simply, it is like a child going into a restaurant and stating, "I shall simply eat what tastes good." The Buddhists have an effective response to this kind of arrogance. They say that what they offer is enlightenment, and since the person inquiring about it does so precisely because he is not enlightened, he must first of all recognize his own lack of enlightenment. An unenlightened person, the Buddhists say, is deluded and thus will choose on the basis of his or her own delusions. Thus a valid tradition, with insightful teachers and authentic practices, is required in order to first diminish and then remove the delusion.

Gnosis is not the same thing as information, although Gnosticism, the vehicle of gnosis, may contain some information. Yet even here one must be careful. Gnostic information is quite different from most other information. It contains myth, visionary insight, psychospiritual stimuli, magical processes, and much more. To treat such material as a compendium of data, pure and simple, would be disastrous. The Gnostic tradition in part exists to make this kind of information assimilable to the mind untrained in Gnostic images, realizations, and language. To set oneself above a tradition that has its own strategies, its own way of seeing reality, and its own spiritual practices is futile and foolish.

Our age is heavily saturated with information and yet ever ravenous for more. It seems that often the more information we amass, the less real our lives become. People are baffled by the technology upon which they depend, and often they are just as baffled by the information they receive through this same technology. Addicts of the information age, we frequently forget that there is another kind of knowledge possible, one in which saying less frequently means knowing more and the rapture of vision replaces the greed for facts. For gnosis has seldom offered facts or even theories; it has always offered experience. In a world in which information becomes obsolete in hours, it may be this kind of informing insight that is most urgently needed.

From Daylight to Midnight Sun

At the beginning of this book, the night sky was used as a metaphor for the light of gnosis in contrast to earthly darkness. It might be useful here, at the conclusion of our study, to expand the metaphor to include the contrast of the daytime and nighttime skies. In the light of day, physical objects are illumined with great clarity. The mundane activities of life require just such clarity of vision. On the other hand, our subtle and more far-seeing night vision is overwhelmed by that very clarity. The celestial luminaries, though present, are hidden by the bright light of day; it is only seldom that we see the contours of the moon in the daytime, while the light of the stars is totally hidden. When the glare of the sun vanishes and the night sky reappears, the objects close at hand here on the earth become shadowy, while the light of the stars light-years away from us strikes our eyes again.

Imagine a world, a reality, that denies itself the vision of the night sky and affirms only the sunlight. Cut off from the vision of the stars, the inhabitants would experience only the sharp contrasts of the daylight world and thus only the mundane, which means primarily the physical. More disastrous, the stimulus to the imagination offered by the light of the stars would be absent. No one would be able to envision a world of boundless light to which the seeming perforations of the black veil appear to bear testimony.

Ours is a world of such denial. Since the Renaissance, our civilization has increasingly committed itself to a worldview based on the daylight world of physical data and on the rational theories that can be deduced from them. We are trapped in the harsh, sun-drenched world of daylight consciousness where we gather more and more facts that, paradoxically, still do not add up to greater happiness. We learn more and more about less and less. Robbed of the Gnostic vision of the night sky with its mysterious lights, we have a disturbingly incomplete understanding of the nonmaterial aspect of our experiences. We seem to be stranded in near-time and near-space, caught in a spiritual myopia of momentous proportion and consequences.

THE GODS THAT FAILED

In a culture that denies the light that shines from beyond this world, people devise means of this-worldly salvation. In the nineteenth and early twentieth centuries, we were driven to believe that socioeconomic doctrines of change would lead to a glorious denouement of human history. Karl Marx had set out to save the world by way of politics wedded to economics; his latter-day disciples Stalin, Mao Tse-tung, and Pol Pot became the most efficient exterminators of their fellow humans known to history. Hitler devised salvation through race and territorial expansion and brought suffering and death to some fifty million people, including his own countrymen. Today, at the beginning of the twenty-first century, we are gradually becoming convinced that for at least two hundred years we have been deceived and abused by political theorists whose activities have brought suffering instead of promised earthly paradise. The god of political salvation has been revealed as a god that has failed.

Another avenue to secular salvation that is in a certain sense a god that has failed us is science. While science has increased our knowledge of the physical world and given us tools for its mastery, it has by no means redeemed us from our existential predicament. The word *science* is derived from the Latin word *scientia*, meaning "knowledge." This is a different sense of knowledge than the word *gnosis* conveys. Gnosis is not primarily scientific or rational in nature. The Greeks in their rather precise manner distinguished between scientific knowledge (as in "he knows chemistry") and gnosis, which is knowledge derived through experience (as in "she knows me").

Another god that is failing us is the god of environmentalism. We are alarmed by the continued growth of technology and have turned into anxious defenders of the natural world—or as we paradoxically call it, the environment. "Environment" is an anthropocentric term since it defines the natural world as something that surrounds human beings. Yet assuming a vaguely pantheistic sense of saving nature or the planet is not the equivalent of saving our souls and spirits. If our inner essence remains polluted, if our consciousness remains inadequate, will a clean environment save us from our own obtuseness and existential malaise? Will solving what some predict is the coming ecocrisis solve or even ease the crisis in our minds and hearts?

Western civilization, especially since the eighteenth and nineteenth centuries, has discovered an enormous amount about the world around us. At the same time, we remain quite in the dark concerning the worlds within us and beyond us. These worlds are at times summed up under the term *consciousness*. It has been said, and justly so, that consciousness is not science's strong point. Even psychology, particularly depth psychology, which attained such prominence in the twentieth century, failed to build a truly effective bridge to science. Freud desired nothing more than to have psychoanalysis recognized as a "new science," yet after the passing of a century his desire remains unfulfilled.

While there is a discipline of study named "consciousness studies," a science of consciousness does not exist. Consciousness is difficult to investigate with scientific procedures and methods, primarily because it responds poorly to the scientific principle of the repeatable experiment. The near failure of the discipline of parapsychology is perhaps the best example. The results of experiments in telepathy and related ESP powers become less and less conclusive as they are repeated.

How do we know that consciousness exists? We know it only by a kind of personal experience that depends less on repeatable experiment and more on the enhancement of a certain mode of perception that can access consciousness. In short, when dealing with consciousness, we are dealing with the realm of gnosis. This was certainly Jung's recognition, which led to his ingenious joining of psychology with both gnosis and Gnosticism. The ancient Gnostics, as Jung recognized, made singular discoveries in the realm of consciousness precisely because they employed modes of perception that were not bound by standards of the ego and its rational, extroverted tendencies.

It is only fair to comment that science has gradually acquired features that point beyond itself, even toward consciousness. Theoretical physics, in particular, has ventured into realms that are more metaphysical in nature than physical. Still, only a small number of qualified scientists take the metaphysical dimensions of their disciplines seriously. The authors who proclaim the presence of a kind of Tao in physics, or other branches of science, are for the most part popularizers whose standing in the scientific community is at best negligible. All the while, the general public, even its educated portion, lives in a

Newtonian and Darwinian world where Einstein, Planck, and their fellows might as well never have existed. Applied science is undoubtedly based on theories that carry metaphysical implications, but these implications are of little interest to the person enjoying the blessings of an ever more sophisticated technology. While it pains one to admit it, in terms of consciousness and therefore of gnosis, science has turned out to be another god that has failed.

The gods listed here that have failed are but some of a much larger number that pretend to salvific power. All are doomed to failure because the entire notion of secular salvation is flawed. What are truly at fault are not the individual inadequacies of the modalities and means. We need to recognize that our essential and abiding needs cannot be satisfied by purely earthly and human resources. The daylight of earthbound thinking is simply inadequate to the task; what we need is another light, one that shines from beyond this world.

Encountering the Gnostic

Gnostics have always been aware of a fundamental predicament that besets us in this world and have identified it as the absence of gnosis. The prophet Hosea, one of the more Gnostic figures of the Old Testament, blames the absence of divine gnosis (knowledge of God) for the misery of not only humans but all creation:

> There is no fidelity, no tenderness, *no knowledge of God* in this country. . . . This is why the country is in mourning, and all who live in it pine away, even the wild animals and the birds of heaven; the fish of the sea themselves are perishing. (Hos. 4.2–3; emphasis added)

This Gnostic point of view is in radical conflict with two ways of viewing the relationship among the Divine, human beings, and the natural world. The first proposes that the human is the source of all values, that the natural world is merely an instrument of human objectives, and that God, if he exists at all, is irrelevant. (This position was perhaps first articulated, in modest form, by Francis Bacon, and became prominent during the Enlightenment.) The second and more recent position proposes that the natural world is the source of all values, that the human being is an intruder into the universal ecosystem, and that God, if he exists at all, is immanent in nature and, in fact, indistinguishable from it. In the Gnostic view, neither the human being nor the natural order can be the source of all values because both are radically alienated from the Divine, where true value resides. Only when human consciousness reaches out across the abyss of separation and contacts the Divine can true values be perceived.

The Gnostic, who in his or her soul and spirit has overcome this alienation from the Divine, is a stranger to the world and to other humans. Meeting with a true Gnostic means meeting a stranger. We may meet such a person indirectly, by way of reading Gnostic scriptures, or directly, by meeting a contemporary Gnostic. In both cases one has met a stranger who communicates strange ideas. But if we engage in creative interaction with this stranger, the stranger may become a friend on whose insight we can rely when it comes to spiritual matters that elude our grasp. Those who have traveled the road ahead of us to the far country are usually qualified to give us directions. The meeting thus may be a promising one.

Again—drawing on an image used by both Mani and the Buddha—the Gnostic is like a boatman who rows out to meet us and help us get to the other shore. The Gnostic tells us that he is acquainted with the territory on the far shore and assures us that great wonders lie in wait for us there. He also reminds us that in order to board his ferry boat we will have to leave the terra firma of our present habitat. This habitat differs with each individual. Secular skeptics may have to let go of the comforts of their lack of spiritual commitment; the devoutly religious may have to transvalue their religious ideals, particularly their concepts of God; the fainthearted may have to muster a certain existential courage to set out on a great adventure. And, perhaps most significantly, the habitué of the New Age spiritual supermarket may need to leave the facile superficiality of that milieu and commit to a demanding process of conscious self-development coupled with a very different worldview.

Gnostic scriptures have identified the human predicament as one of ignorance, sleep, drunkenness, or forgetfulness. These constituents of our sad condition come in many guises. We are like animals so habituated to their confinement that they refuse to leave their cages once the doors are opened. The sleep and stupor of our present existence seem preferable to the kind of freedom brought by gnosis. We seldom question the consensus worldview of our culture or the dogmas of our religion, yet we now seem to question the teachings derived from Gnostic insight. Some of this questioning is, of course, useful. But we need to question not only Gnostics and their teachings but the questioner also. Are we unwilling to contemplate the Gnostic postulates because they contradict what the majority think? How many of the cherished beliefs that stand in the way of our willingness to accept Gnostic ideas are really no more than untested assumptions foisted on us by our society?

It was true two thousand years ago and is still true today that, to the large majority of humankind, Gnosticism is disturbing and at times even infuriating; it represents a challenge to what most have believed and practiced. Those who are determined to make more of this world than it is are horrified by Gnosticism and its sober recognition that secular salvation is not possible. The world cannot be lifted up by its own bootstraps, whether these are envisioned as political, economic, scientific, or ecological in nature. What the world needs is something outside of itself—a wisdom, an interior knowledge that transcends the boundaries of the planet and of the cosmos. Such a position appears detached and otherworldly to the modern or postmodern mind, obsessed with the virtues of social change. The upholders of the status quo in society also tend to view the Gnostic with a jaundiced eye. How could someone who calls the Creator foul names, who perceives a flaw in all things that concern creation, and who does not view the commandments of either religion or of society as salvific be anything but a destabilizing force in society?

Those, however, who have come to recognize life as tragic, who have felt the forlornness and alienation of their consciousness amidst their own powerlessness, are far more likely to be responsive to the Gnostic message. Those who have suffered enough in their earthly lives and who have managed to add a maximum amount of consciousness to their suffering, so that they now possess the necessary right intent and sincerity, are likely to listen to the strange and ancient voice of the Gnostic that calls to them—nowadays with renewed strength. These are the souls and minds who are likely to turn their gaze from the harsh daylight of rationality and extroversion to the mysterious luminosity of the night sky, where the light of gnosis may be perceived. For them, the encounter with the Gnostic teachings is beneficial. The light of the stars, so long blotted out by the daylight, reappears, and the dark shadows cast by the daylight recede. And amidst the stars, the mysterious midnight sun seen by the initiates of old makes its welcome appearance.

APPENDIX A

A GNOSTIC READING LIST

This is not a comprehensive bibliography of works on Gnosticism; it is intended to serve simply as a guide for readers seeking books that merit attention. The majority of these books are in print, and most are available at a university library; however, several important books mentioned here are out of print, and a few are difficult to find even in a good library.

INTRODUCTORY READINGS

Holroyd, Stuart. *The Elements of Gnosticism*. Shaftesbury, Dorset, Eng., and Rockport, Mass.: Element Books, 1994.

> An excellent, brief introduction to the teachings, history, and literature of Gnosticism. The approach is sympathetic, with emphasis on the relevance of Gnosticism for today.

Pagels, Elaine. *The Gnostic Gospels*. New York: Random House, 1978.

> A popular classic, introducing the Nag Hammadi scriptures and Gnosticism within a useful historical context. Perhaps the first major book to be free of the anti-Gnostic heresiological bias.

Seymour-Smith, Martin. *Gnosticism: The Path of Inner Knowledge*. San Francisco: Harper San Francisco, 1996.

> A small coffee table book, attractively illustrated in color, with a mildly sympathetic treatment of the subject. Brief but informative.

Singer, June. *Knowledge of the Heart: Gnostic Secrets of Inner Wisdom.* Rockport, Mass.: Element, 1999.

Delightful labor of love of Gnosis by a noted Jungian. Consists of Gnostic sacred texts arranged for reading according to the monastic hours and days of the week. Commentaries of Jungian and Gnostic inspiration are appended to the texts. An instrument for deepening of one's gnosis. (This book was previously published as *A Gnostic Book of Hours: Keys to Inner Wisdom.* San Francisco: Harper San Francisco, 1992.)

INTERMEDIATE READINGS

Churton, Tobias. *The Gnostics.* London: Weidenfeld and Nicolson, 1987.

A comprehensive, well researched, and objective study, encompassing Gnostic teachings and literature. Includes a useful chronological table. (This book was written to accompany a television documentary, *The Gnostics,* produced in Great Britain by Boarder Television in 1987.)

Dart, John. *The Laughing Savior: The Discovery and Significance of the Nag Hammadi Gnostic Library.* New York: Harper & Row, 1976.

Journalistic, slightly superficial sampling of the Nag Hammadi scriptures, with mildly informative contextual information.

Doresse, Jean. *The Secret Books of the Egyptian Gnostic: An Introduction to the Gnostic Coptic Manuscripts Discovered at Chenoboskion.* New York: Viking, 1960.

Personal account by one of the discoverers of the Nag Hammadi scriptures. Includes an early translation of the Gospel of Thomas. The author manifests an anti-Gnostic bias.

Grant, Robert M. *Gnosticism and Early Christianity*. New York: Harper Torchbooks, 1966.

> A moderately useful treatment of the subject, marred by the negative attitude of the author, rooted in a heresiological bias.

Guirdham, Arthur. *The Great Heresy*. Jersey, Eng.: Neville Spearman, 1977.

> Study of the teachings of the medieval Gnostics known as the Cathars. Part 1 of the book is highly informative and insightful. Part 2 is based on alleged communications from discarnate entities and therefore is of questionable value.

Hoeller, Stephan A. *Jung and the Lost Gospels*. Wheaton, IL: Theosophical Publishing House, Quest Books, 1989.

> A study showing the relationship of Jung's psychology to the principal Gnostic myths and to four of the Nag Hammadi gospels.

Jonas, Hans. *The Gnostic Religion*. Boston: Beacon, 1958, 2001.

> A classic work, employing existential principles of analysis to Gnostic teachings (the author was a student of Heidegger). Contains many valuable quotations, including many from Mandaean and Manichaean sources. Written before the publication of the Nag Hammadi scriptures, it contains only scant references to these sources.

Lacarriere, Jacques. *The Gnostics*. New York: Dutton, 1977. Reprint, San Francisco: City Lights, 1989.

> A poetic meditation on Gnosticism and Gnostic teachings. The author's antiestablishment, left-wing orientation needs to be discounted, but it contains useful information and is sympathetic to Gnosticism. Includes a worthwhile foreword by Lawrence Durrell.

Merkur, Dan. *Gnosis: An Esoteric Tradition of Mystical Visions and Unions.* Albany: State University of New York Press, 1993.

Startlingly creative and insightful work that sees Gnosticism as originating in a certain kind of spiritual experience akin to C. G. Jung's "active imagination." Includes cognate material from Christian, Jewish, and Islamic mysticism. Well documented and readable.

Oldenbourg, Zoe. *Massacre at Montségur: A History of the Albigensian Crusade.* New York: Minerva, 1968.

A classic work on the bloody war and persecution of the medieval Gnostic (Cathar) religion in the Languedoc, France. The first historical work to unmask this persecution in its full horror. Written by a noted medievalist and historical novelist.

O'Shea, Stephen. *The Perfect Heresy: The Revolutionary Life and Death of the Medieval Cathars.* New York: Walker, 2000.

A readable, popular account of the Cathar phenomenon and of the Albigensian Crusade. The author is sympathetic to the Cathar cause.

Perkins, Pheme. *The Gnostic Dialogue: The Early Church and the Crisis of Gnosticism.* New York: Paulist Press, 1980.

Informative study, marred by the author's Roman Catholic bias and obvious attempt to counteract the pro-Gnostic effect of Elaine Pagel's work, *The Gnostic Gospels.*

Rudolph, Kurt. *Gnosis: The Nature and History of Gnosticism.* San Francisco: Harper & Row, 1983.

Detailed and scholarly exposition, equally valuable to scholar and lay person. The author's point of view is objective and in the main uninfluenced by heresiological bias. Includes excellent documentation, as well as Mandaean materials obtained by the author in his personal research.

Spierenburg, H. J., ed. *H. P. Blavatsky: On the Gnostics*. San Diego, Calif.: Point Loma Publications, 1994.

Compilation of the writings of various lengths on the Gnostics by the seminal figure of the nineteenth-century occult revival. It proves Blavatsky's excellent insight into matters Gnostic, as well as the intimate compatibility between Gnosticism and modern Theosophy.

Advanced Readings

Blackman, E. C. *Marcion and His Influence*. London: SPCK, 1948. Reprint, New York: Ames, 1978.

Classic study of Marcion's teachings and their impact on various disciplines, including biblical criticism. Arguably the most complete work on Marcion yet written.

Culianu, Ioan P. *The Tree of Gnosis: Gnostic Mythology from Early Christianity to Modern Nihilism*. San Francisco: Harper, 1992.

Highly imaginative but somewhat immature study of the Gnostic tradition, with a strong historical emphasis. Creative but turgid.

Filoramo, Giovanni. *A History of Gnosticism*. Cambridge, Mass.: Blackwell, 1990.

Excellent and sympathetic study of Gnosticism, including insightful exegeses of Gnostic scriptures. One of the best scholarly works available.

Hedrick, Charles W., and Robert Hodgson, eds. *Nag Hammadi Gnosticism and Early Christianity*. Peabody, Mass.: Hendrickson, 1986.

Several valuable studies, primarily concerning the Nag Hammadi collection of Gnostic scriptures, by fourteen noted scholars of this field.

King, C. W. *The Gnostics and Their Remains, Ancient and Medieval.* 1887. Reprint, San Diego, Calif..: Wizards Bookshelf, 1982.

A classic nineteenth-century work, depicting and explaining primarily items of talismanic art of the Gnostic tradition.

King, Karen L., ed. *Images of the Feminine in Gnosticism.* Philadelphia: Fortress, 1988.

Transactions of a conference bearing the same title, held in 1985 at the Institute of Antiquity and Christianity in Claremont, California. Contains thirty-two essays and responses by scholars. The contents are of mixed value.

Klimkeit, Hans-Joachim. *Gnosis on the Silk Road: Gnostic Texts from Central Asia.* San Francisco: Harper, 1993.

A useful brief introduction to Manichaeanism, along with a large collection of beautiful Manichaean texts obtained from materials uncovered in Central Asia during the last century.

Lieu, Samuel N. C. *Manichaeism in the Late Roman Empire and Medieval China.* 2nd rev. ed. Tubingen: Mohr, 1992.

A highly detailed discussion of Manichaeanism, and perhaps the best current modern work on the subject. Of particular importance, this work includes very comprehensive notes and a bibliography listing essentially every important extant work on Manichaeanism.

———. *Manichaeism in Mesopotamia and the Roman East.* Leiden: Brill, 1994.

A collection of Lieu's essays, most highly specialized in nature, which complement his previous work, *Manichaeism in the Late Roman Empire and Medieval China.*

————. *Manichaeism in Central Asia and China*. Leiden: Brill, 1998.

A further collection of Lieu's essays, again highly specialized in nature, which complement his previous works.

Lupieri, Edmondo. *The Mandaeans: The Last Gnostics*. Grand Rapids, Mich.: Eerdmans, 2002.

One of the very few works available on the Mandaean religion. Well researched and readable. Contains numerous translations of Mandaean scriptures. Highly recommended.

Mead, G. R. S. *Simon Magus: An Essay*. London: Theosophical Publishing Society, 1892.

Pagels, Elaine. H. *The Johannine Gospel in Gnostic Exegesis: Heracleon's Commentary on John*. Nashville and New York: Abingdon, 1973.

Useful exposition of Valentinian interpretations of the Gospel of John, including material on John the Baptizer.

————. *The Gnostic Paul: Gnostic Exegesis of the Pauline Letters*. Philadelphia: Trinity Press International, 1975.

An examination of the Valentinian Gnostic reading of the Pauline letters, offering a new perspective on Pauline studies.

————. *Adam, Eve, and the Serpent*. New York: Random House, 1988.

The impact of the first three chapters of Genesis on the political thought of Christendom. Chapter 3 is of singular interest to Gnostic studies.

Perkins, Pheme. *Gnosticism and the New Testament*. Minneapolis: Fortress, 1993.

A scholarly account of the interaction of Gnosticism and New Testament Christianity. Primarily useful to readers with an interest in a biblical perspective in regard to Gnosticism.

Petrement, Simone. *A Separate God: The Christian Origins of Gnosticism*. San Francisco: Harper, 1990.

An important study, viewing Gnosticism as a purely Christian phenomenon. The somewhat obscure style of the author makes it slightly difficult reading.

Roukema, Reimer. *Gnosis and Faith in Early Christianity*. Harrisburg, Pa.: Trinity Press International, 1999.

A basic introduction to the relationship of Gnosticism to early Christianity. The author represents a Calvinist Protestant position and relies heavily on the heresiologist patristic sources. The work contains a rare exposition of the convergences between Gnosticism and Plato, Philo, and other Platonic teachers.

Stoyanov, Yuri. *The Other God: Dualist Religions from Antiquity to the Cathar Heresy*. New Haven: Yale University Press, 2000.

An excellent historical study tracing the possible origins of Gnosticism to Egyptian and Zoroastrian sources and showing unusually keen insight into the Bogomil and Cathar religions.

Welburn, Andrew. *Mani, the Angel and the Column of Glory*. Edinburgh: Floris, 1998.

A useful annotated anthology of Manichaean texts edited and presented by a distinguished scholar. Contains some texts not frequently available. The perspective of the author is considerably influenced by the teachings of Rudolph Steiner.

Editions of Gnostic Scriptures

Foerster, Werner, ed. *Gnosis, A Selection of Gnostic Texts.* Vol. 2. *Coptic and Mandean Sources.* Oxford: Clarendon, 1974.

> The second part contains a valuable selection of writings of the Mandaeans of Iraq. This volume is easier to obtain than other books on this tradition.

Gardner, Iain. *The Kephalaia of the Teacher: The Edited Coptic Manichaean Texts in Translation with Commentary.* Leiden: Brill, 1995.

> Contains one of the best available detailed introductory discussions of Manichaeanism, along with an excellent translation of the Kephalaia, a collection of the "oral teachings of Mani to his disciples."

The Gospel according to Thomas: With Complementary Texts. Santa Barbara, Calif.: Concord Grove, 1983.

> An elegant translation of the Gospel of Thomas and of the Apocryphon of John, The Gospel of Truth, and the "Hymn of the Pearl," along with a useful introduction representing a modern Theosophical perspective.

Greenlees, Duncan. *The Gospel of the Gnostics.* Adyar, Madras: Theosophical Publishing House, 1958.

> This volume appeared as volume 13 of the World Gospel Series and includes a superb selection of Gnostic writings, though it was published before and therefore excludes the Nag Hammadi scriptures. Includes a fine introduction, along with extended commentaries on the scriptures. Unfortunately, this work is long out of print and extremely hard to find.

————. *The Gospel of the Prophet Mani*. Adyar, Madras: Theosophical Publishing House, 1958.

This appeared as volume 12 of the World Gospel Series and includes perhaps the most useful selection of Manichaean writings in print. Excellent introduction and commentaries. Unfortunately, this work is long out of print and extremely hard to find.

Layton, Bentley. *The Gnostic Scriptures*. Garden City, N.Y.: Doubleday, & Co., 1987.

Outstanding translations with commentaries of some of the scriptures from the Nag Hammadi collection, along with a large number of quotations from and references to Gnostic sources by heresiological church fathers. An excellent, scholarly introduction to the study of Gnostic scriptures.

Mead, G. R. S. *Fragments of a Faith Forgotten: A Contribution to the Study of the Origins of Christianity*. 1900. Reprint, Kila, Mont.: Kessinger, 1991.

Mead's superb exposition of virtually all Gnostic materials extant prior to the Nag Hammadi discovery.

————. *The Hymn of Jesus*. 1907. Reprint, Wheaton, Ill.: Theosophical Publishing House, 1973.

————. *Pistis Sophia: A Gnostic Miscellany*. 1896. Reprint, Blautvelt, N.Y.: Garber, 1973.

The most readable translation of major portions of the Books of the Savior (Askew Codex), with excerpts of related literature and valuable commentaries. The major source on Valentinian Sophiology.

Meyer, Marvin. *The Gospel of Thomas: The Hidden Sayings of Jesus.* San Francisco: HarperSanFrancisco, 1992.

The latest translation of the most accessible Gnostic scripture. The translator's introduction and an interpretive essay by Harold Bloom serve as useful entry points both for the study of this gospel and for Gnosticism in general.

————. *The Secret Teachings of Jesus: Four Gnostic Gospels.* New York: Random House, 1984.

A fine translation of four texts from the Nag Hammadi collection: The Gospel of James; The Gospel of Thomas; The Book of Thomas; and The Secret Book of John. Includes a useful introduction.

Miller, Robert J., ed. *The Complete Gospels.* San Francisco: Harper, 1994.

A nice collection of all extant "gospel" texts—canonical, Gnostic, and other noncanonical writings—in new translations. The introductions and notes are particularly clear and useful.

Robinson, James M., ed. *The Nag Hammadi Library in English.* 3rd rev. ed. San Francisco: Harper, 1988.

The epochal translation of the entire Nag Hammadi library, discovered in 1945. The revised 1988 edition lacks the index of the previous edition and contains an indifferent afterword.

Schmidt, Carl, ed. *Pistis Sophia.* Leiden: Brill, 1978.

Useful alternative to Mead's more readable translation; accurate and scholarly.

————. *The Books of Jeu and the Untitled Text in the Bruce Codex.* Leiden: Brill, 1978.

The only available translation of the content of the Bruce Codex. The Books of Jeu are invaluable as sources of Gnostic theurgy. Unfortunately the translation of the words of the diagrams in The Books of Jeu are inadequate.

Appendix B

A Brief Gnostic Glossary

The following is a brief list of Gnostic words. It contains both names of mythic entities appearing in Gnostic scriptures and terms denoting concepts in Gnostic usage. The list is far from exhaustive and is designed as a basic aid to reading and comprehending Gnostic literature.

Abraxas: (barbarous word) The name given by Gnostics to the redeemed archon, a son of Sophia, who came to occupy the position of ruler of the seventh heaven. He is depicted as a being with the head of a rooster, the torso of a man, and legs fashioned as serpents. Abraxas is depicted on many Gnostic amulets discovered after the passing of the Gnostic movements of Alexandria and Syria.

Achamoth: (Heb.) An anagram of Chokmah, meaning wisdom; usually associated with the lower aspect of Sophia.

Aeon: (Gk.) An emanated aspect of the Divine Reality. Aeons are often represented as pairs (male and female) joined and balancing each other.

Anthropos: (Gk.) Man. The heavenly prototype of humanity, emanated from the Ultimate Reality.

Archon: (Gk.) Ruler. An inferior cosmic being ruling over and imposing limitations on creation.

Barbarous words: Words not originating in any known language, usually consisting of vowels and frequently used in Gnostic scriptures and rituals as words of power.

Barbelo: (Heb.) The name of a feminine aspect of the Divine; at times regarded as God the Mother.

Christos: (Gk.) The Anointed. In Gnostic usage, a heavenly Aeon who at one point in time conjoins with Jesus.

Cosmos: (Gk.) The system. The systematized appearance of reality constellated by creative agencies of limited intelligence and benevolence.

Demiurge: (Gk.) The fashioner of the lower world of manifestation. He is the chief of the archons and is of limited wisdom and imperfect.

Emanation: (Ln.) The Gnostic way of envisioning creation in its original aspect. All worlds and beings are originally emanated from the Divine Reality and are only later fashioned into cosmic systems by the Demiurge.

Gospel: (OE *godspell* "good news" translated from **Ln.** *evangelium* from **Gk.** *evangelion*) In Gnostic usage, any scripture designed to advance the enlightenment, or gnosis, of humanity.

Gnosis: (Gk.) Salvific knowing, arrived at intuitively but facilitated by various stimuli, including the teachings and mysteries brought to humans by messengers of divinity from outside the cosmos.

IALDABAOTH: (barbarous word) Possibly meaning "the childish god." A name for the Demiurge.

Logos: (Gk.) The Word of the Most High God. In Gnostic scriptures, also a title of Jesus.

Manda: (Gk.) Gnosis. The word from which is derived the name of the Mandaeans, the only indisputably direct successors of the ancient Gnostics, who still reside in the Middle East.

Pistis: (Gk.) Faith. A quality of spiritual trust, primarily as placed in one's gnosis, or intuitive knowing. A quality exemplified in Faithful Sophia because of her abiding trust in the Light.

Pleroma: (Gk.) Fullness. Denoting the plenum, or transcendental field of Divine Reality, from which, by emanation, all manifest existence has come forth and where it is destined to return.

Pneuma: (Gk.) Spirit. The highest principle resident in the human being. *Pneuma*, *psyche*, and *hyle* together constitute the trinity of spirit, soul, and material body.

Saclas: (Aram.) The fool; the blind fool. One of the names of the Demiurge.

Sophia: (Gk.) Greek form of the Hebrew *Chokmah*, denoting Wisdom. In Gnosticism, as in some Christian sources, this is the proper name of a transcendental being coming forth from the Most High God. Gnostic sources describe her fall from the Fullness, her agonizing journey in the chaotic lower worlds, and her restoration to her original place.

Soter: (Gk.) Savior, redeemer. Used most frequently as a title for Christ.

BIBLIOGRAPHY OF MODERN BOOKS CITED
OTHER THAN THOSE IN APPENDIX A

Berdyaev, Nikolay. *The Beginning and the End.* Gloucester, Mass.: P. Smith, 1970.

Blavatsky, Helena Petrovna. *Isis Unveiled: A Master-Key to the Mysteries of Ancient and Modern Science and Theology.* 2 vols. 1877. Reprint; Wheaton, Ill.: Theosophical Publishing House, 1972.

———. *The Secret Doctrine: The Synthesis of Science, Religion, and Philosophy.* 2 vols. 1888. Reprint in 3 vols.; Adyar, Madras, India: Theosophical Publishing House, 1978.

Bloom, Harold. "A Reading." In *The Gospel of Thomas: The Hidden Sayings of Jesus,* trans. Marvin Meyer. San Francisco: HarperSanFrancisco, 1992.

———. *Omens of Millennium: The Gnosis of Angels, Dreams, and Resurrection.* New York: Riverhead Books, 1996.

Buber, Martin. *Eclipse of God: Studies in the Relation between Religion and Philosophy.* New York: Harper, 1952.

Cavendish, Richard, ed. *Man, Myth, and Magic: The Illustrated Encyclopedia of the Supernatural.* New York: Marshall Cavendish, 1970.

Drower, Ethel Stefana, Lady. *The Canonical Prayerbook of the Mandaeans.* Leiden: Brill, 1959.

————. *The Mandaeans of Iraq and Iran: Their Cults, Customs, Magic, Legends, and Folklore*. Oxford: Clarendon, 1937.

Ehrenfeld, David W. *The Arrogance of Humanism*. New York: Oxford University Press, 1975.

Huxley, Aldous. *The Perennial Philosophy*. London: Chatto and Windus, 1937.

John Paul II, Pope. *Crossing the Threshold of Hope*. New York: Knopf, 1994.

Jung, Carl Gustav. *Memories, Dreams, Reflections*. New York: Random House, 1963.

Kerényi, Karl, and C. G. Jung. *Essays on a Science of Mythology: The Myth of the Divine Child and the Mysteries of Eleusis*. New York: Pantheon, 1949.

Krishnamurti, Jiddu. *At the Feet of the Master*. 1910. Reprint as *At the Feet of the Master and Toward Discipleship*; Wheaton, Ill.: Theosophical Publishing House, Quest Books, 2001.

Magre, Maurice. *The Return of the Magi*. London: Allen, 1931.

Patai, Raphael. *The Hebrew Goddess*. New York: Ktav Publishing House, 1968.

Quispel, Gilles. *Gnosis als Weltreligion*. Zurich: Origo, 1951.

Runciman, Steven, Sir. *Medieval Manichee: A Study of the Christian Dualist Heresy*. Cambridge: University Press, 1947.

Taubes, Jacob. *Gnosis und Politik*. Munich: Kösel, 1959.

Voegelin, Eric. *New Science of Politics: An Introduction*. Chicago: University of Chicago Press, 1960.

————.*Order and History*. Baton Rouge: Louisiana State University Press, 1974.

————. *Science, Politics, and Gnosticism: Two Essays*. Chicago: Regnery, 1968.

Waugh, Evelyn. *The Diaries of Evelyn Waugh*. Ed. Michael Davie. London: Weidenfeld and Nicolson, 1975.

Weber, Max. *The Protestant Ethic and the Spirit of Capitalism*. London: Allen and Unwin, 1930.

Williams, Michael Allen. *Rethinking "Gnosticism": An Argument for Dismantling a Dubious Category*. Princeton, N.J.: Princeton University Press, 1996.

INDEX

Related Quest Titles